Ancient Salt

Ancient Salt

Essays on Poets, Poetry, and the Modern World

ANDREW FRISARDI

RESOURCE *Publications* · Eugene, Oregon

Resource Publications
An Imprint of Wipf and Stock Publishers
199 W. 8th Ave., Suite 3
Eugene, OR 97401

www.wipfandstock.com

PAPERBACK ISBN: 978-1-6667-3916-9
HARDCOVER ISBN: 978-1-6667-3917-6
EBOOK ISBN: 978-1-6667-3918-3

JUNE 21, 2022 10:34 AM

For John Carey

CONTENTS

Preface

M Y essays in *Ancient Salt* are about several modern and contemporary poets—British, American, and Italian. I offer close readings of these poets, and consider their work in light of the challenges of living and writing amid the extraordinary transformations of the modern era. Some of the poets are religious, some are agnostic or perhaps atheist, but all of them articulate a human-poetic response to modernity: its pluralism, mobility, scientific discoveries, innovations, and unprecedented global awareness; as well as its rootlessness, fragmentation, dehumanizing mechanization, materialism, environmental catastrophes, and even systematic genocide. Needless to say, many if not all poets could be approached from the perspective of how they express or adapt to their time and place. Most of the poets in this book are ones whose creative responses to the modern world have been explicit and fundamental to their work.

The subjects of the essays are: Orkney-Scottish visionary poet Edwin Muir (1887–1959); Italian hermetic poet Giuseppe Ungaretti (1888–1970); Irish poet-dramatist W. B. Yeats (1865–1939); Welsh Christian poet Vernon Watkins (1906–1968); English poet and Blake scholar Kathleen Raine (1908–2003); English-cosmopolitan poet Peter Russell (1921–2003); American poet and Alaskan homesteader John Haines (1924–2011); English poet and Jungian Richard Berengarten (formerly Burns) (1943–); and American poet-critic and Tasmanian expat David Mason (1954–). Since Peter Russell is the least likely to be known to contemporary readers of poetry in English, I've included both an essay about him and an interview I conducted with him in person a couple of years before his death.

Preface

I decided that the simplest and thematically most interesting way to arrange the essays was chronologically by the poets' birth years. The one exception to this is the Yeats essay, which would go first chronologically but which better fits the arc of this book as the third chapter.

ANDREW FRISARDI

May 2, 2022

THE GOOD LIFE OF EDWIN MUIR

Muir [was] concerned with imagination not only in order that there
may be good poetry, but in order that man himself may survive.

—THOMAS MERTON

T HE EVOLUTION OF ART isn't as linear as modern art history makes
it seem. Unlike science, which develops incrementally and—in
theory at least—always improves on what came before, art often
advances by revisiting (while not mechanically repeating, of course) previous styles and values. Such unprogressiveness implies a broader definition
of contemporaneity than our own time generally allows. The postmodern
aesthetic tends to be blinkered in its judgment of what makes art relevant
to contemporary life. Many seek no more from art than a mirror of what
surrounds us in the present: cynical commercialism, built-in obsolescence,
and virtual unreality.

In such a climate it isn't surprising that a poet like Edwin Muir has
faded from view. Until the early 2000s or so, Graywolf Press kept his absorbing *Autobiography* in print; as well as *The Estate of Poetry*, Muir's 1955–
56 Charles Eliot Norton lectures on the relationship between poetry and
society. These books were later taken up by independent print-on-demand
ventures and can be found online. Muir's *Collected Poems* was last published
in 2003 by Faber, which also issued a *Selected Poems* in 2008. Not since the
early 1960s, however, when writers such as Thomas Merton, Allen Tate,
and Hayden Carruth were paying serious attention to Muir, has his poetry
been discussed much in U.S. journals. One reason for the relative neglect
of Muir's poetry is its traditional, English and ballad-influenced prosody,

which kept it obscure for many years even in Muir's own time, when modernist poetics held sway; and its unironic high seriousness clearly doesn't fit in with the cultural atmosphere of the early twenty-first century.

Muir's style, however, isn't the only or even the greatest difference between him and most of modern and postmodern poetry. Everyone who knows Muir's work knows that he grew up as the son of a peasant farmer in the Orkneys, in one of the last communities in Europe practically untouched by Renaissance and Enlightenment culture—and that his poetry and prose are greatly affected, one might even say determined, by the struggle Muir underwent when circumstances landed him in the middle of several modern industrial and political nightmares. Like T. S. Eliot, Muir believed that contemporaneity includes a relation to the past, but the past to which Muir related his experience was not literary so much as ancestral and organic; "culture" for Muir meant everything from animal husbandry to Dante and Milton. He could afford to be less anxious about the relation of individual talent to tradition precisely because his tradition, while including elements of high culture, was more primary than the latter. It was based on the fundamental relationships between human beings living together in interdependent community with nature. Muir depicts his native community in his *Autobiography*:

> I cannot say how much my idea of a good life was influenced by my early upbringing, but it seems to me that its sins were mere sins of the flesh, which are excusable, and not sins of the spirit. The farmers did not know ambition and the petty torments of ambition; they did not realize what competition was. . . . They helped one another with their work when help was required. . . . They had a culture made up of legend, folk-song, and the poetry and prose of the Bible; they had customs with which they sanctioned their instinctive feelings for the earth; their life was an order, and a good order.[1]

This background explains why, while most other modern writers were, in Ezra Pound's words, writing from a fragmented stream, Muir was still vitally related to the lost world of social and cultural unity. When Muir wrote lines such as "But still from Eden springs the root / As clean as on the starting day," he was expressing a sentiment many writers believed or felt but few could assert with real conviction. So it came about that Muir was

---

1. Muir, *Autobiography*, 65.

one of those poets, rare in any age, whose vocation it was to bear witness to a vision of radical innocence and the fate of it in the world.

Muir's equanimity is surely one of the things that attract his admirers. Though masterful, his writing is not technically flashy; nor does it reflect back to us our existential anxieties and fragmented identities. Rather, a singular quality of Muir's writing is that it reminds us of the possibility of a rooted way of being and thinking. Muir was consistent in his distrust of the modern idea of progress; he warned that, in a culture overdetermined by technological development, outward changes happen so fast that our essential identity becomes "indistinct. . . . The imagination cannot pierce to it as easily as it once could."[2] The constant metamorphosis of outer life brought about by technology obscures the essentials of human experience, which are remarkably consistent over time. In an essay called "The Poetic Imagination," published in *Essays on Literature and Society*, Muir distinguished between technological and human progress:

> Applied science shows us a world of consistent, mechanical progress. Machines give birth to ever new generations of machines, and the new machines are always better and more efficient than the old, and begin where the old left off. . . . But in the world of human beings all is different. . . . Every human being has to begin at the beginning, as his forebears did, with the same difficulties and pleasures, the same temptations, the same problem of good and evil, the same inclination to ask what life means.[3]

Despite the measured tone of this passage, which Muir wrote in his late fifties, his actual, early confrontation with industrialized society was personally calamitous. From his teenage years, when his family was economically forced to move to Glasgow (four of Muir's family, including his parents, died within the next few years), into his mid-thirties, Muir earned a living at various menial jobs, experiencing preunionized labor and modern urban poverty firsthand. One clerical job, for example, forced him to live in a town entirely dominated by the company for which he worked, a factory that burned the bones of slaughtered animals to use the ashes for making glue. Muir describes the freight cars full of bones "festooned by the yellow cable of maggots," and the rank stench of rotting flesh from which it was impossible to escape anywhere in town.[4] It is not surprising

---

2. Muir, "The Poetic Imagination," in *Essays on Literature and Society*, 225.

3. Muir, "The Poetic Imagination," in *Essays on Literature and Society*, 225.

4. Muir, *Autobiography*, 143.

that Muir turned during this period to Nietzsche and socialism, the former, as he realized afterward, providing him with a rationalized fantasy of power in the face of overwhelming, impotent despair; and that the aphorisms he wrote at his desk at work were bitter and ironic, unlike anything he was to write later.

What *is* remarkable is that Muir did not become a social realist, like W. H. Auden, Cecil Day-Lewis, Stephen Spender, and other related British poets during the 1930s, who didn't know anything close to what Muir knew directly about urban poverty. Instead, he applied his genius for symbolic or mythic thought to integrating his childhood and his adult experiences: "One foot in Eden still, I stand / And look across the other land," as he says at the start of the title poem of his last collection, *One Foot in Eden* (1956).[5] Again and again, Muir's poems address the archetypal dichotomy of innocence and innocence lost, often using Bible stories, especially Eden and the Fall, to communicate the sense of a chasm between living in unity with others and with God and nature, and living in isolation, dislocation, and dis-ease. Once he had regained the psychological vantage point of his childhood experience—after undergoing a breakdown in London, subsequent Jungian analysis, and finally leaving Britain with his wife, Willa (the first translator, along with Muir himself, of Kafka)—he referred to it in his writing as the ground or touchstone or prototype-of-wholeness against which he measured contemporary disturbance, flux, and change.

An interesting essay could be written about the animals in Muir's poetry. Farmer's son that he was, he does not depict animals in a Rousseauian wild state, but rather, in terms of humanity's dependence on them. Muir's most widely anthologized poem, "The Horses" (which Eliot referred to as a "great poem of the nuclear age"), treats this theme, and the related one of alienation and reconciliation between human beings and nature, with a masterfully paced narrative and vivid tangible detail. Importantly, Muir wrote this poem in the 1950s, the coldest period of the Cold War; it appears in *One Foot in Eden*. Muir sets up the poem in the first few lines with the contrast between unity and division that will structure the whole piece.

> Barely a twelvemonth after
> The seven days war that put the world to sleep,
> Late in the evening the strange horses came.
> . . .
> By then we had made our covenant with silence,

5. All quotations from Muir's poetry in this essay are taken from *Collected Poems*.

But in the first few days it was so still
We listened to our breathing and were afraid.

And the poem adds that radios and remote communications had gone dead as well. The silence is uncomfortable at first; people don't know what to do with themselves.

The first inkling of reconciliation with the animals is depicted later in this poem with confident simplicity: "Late in the summer the strange horses came." The horses are "strange," it turns out, simply because we estranged ourselves from them. The poem itself makes clear they are not wild, but are old farm horses. In a letter Muir wrote in July 1958 he states that he had wished to emphasize the relationship between the human and the natural world: the horses are "good plough-horses and still have a memory of the world before the war. I try to suggest they are looking for their old human companionship."[6] Yet the speakers of the poem, a collective "we" (a common device in Muir's poetry), respond to the horses' return with fear of their instinctual energy, presumably because the machines with which they replaced them, the "dank sea-monsters" now "moldering away . . . like other loam," did not require them to exercise their capacity for relating to living things. The speakers of the poem, then, don't trust the horses' return.

We did not dare go near them. Yet they waited,
Stubborn and shy, as if they had been sent
By an old command to find our whereabouts
And that long-lost archaic companionship.

With remarkable economy, this passage concretizes the idea of reconciliation; so Muir can conclude the poem with a specific image of renewal: "Our life is changed; their coming our beginning."

This deep acceptance of our inextricable closeness to animals and nature, coupled with esteem for human culture and intellect, is one of the aspects of Muir that makes his work so clear-sighted and sound. Despite his mystical temperament, Muir always maintained a down-to-earth perspective. In his critical writings, he was as likely to appreciate Austen, Thackeray, and Rabelais, as Hölderlin; and he disliked the poet Paul Valéry for being too remote from everyday life. Muir's equanimity and balance made it possible for him to appreciate a very wide range of styles and views; his 1926 volume of critical studies, *Transition*, is remarkable for its insightful and jargon-free characterizations of James Joyce, D. H. Lawrence,

6. Letter to Derek Hawes, July 7, 1958, in Muir, *Selected Letters*, 205.

Virginia Wolff, and others. This tolerance for aesthetic and philosophical views markedly different from his own, along with his knack for illuminating generalization, are qualities that make Muir's critical writings so rich and worthwhile. He never liked the so-called New Criticism, believing it reinforced (because it overintellectualized its subject) the already widening gap between writer and audience. Muir always remains familiar and approachable. At the same time, his poetry has features in common with the symbolist aesthetic that appeals to many metaphysical poets: expressive concentration, interpenetration of idea and image, and sparseness of quotidian detail. Muir's distinctive voice is a blend of earthy directness and visionary idealism; his is a romanticism of the second half of life. As a deeply Christian man, he held to the doctrine of Incarnation as a link between the interior life and practical life; and rebuked John Knox, the Calvinist, for betraying that teaching by keeping the Renaissance, with all its worldly insights, out of Scotland.

For Muir, culture is the zone in which mind and nature, the timeless and the temporal meet and are reconciled. This is why he didn't agree with Auden and other modernists who claimed that poetry is "useless." Useless, yes, if by that we mean *utilitarian*; but incomparably useful when we remember that without art—without *gratuitous beauty*—a society can have no living dialogue with its own depths and heights. Muir believed that one of the tasks of art was to renew the ligatures that keep these connections current and vital, and that civilization itself cannot survive without such renewal.

His own unique brand of political poem—and he wrote some fine ones during the Cold War years—was based on these notions. "The Usurpers" is one of several poems Muir wrote about his experience of postwar Prague, where he was director of the British Council Institute just after World War II, from 1945 to 1948. A Czech writer, a friend of the Muirs, had shown them a photograph of some young Gestapo men, one of whom had interrogated, tortured, and murdered her husband. She also showed her husband's shirt, covered with dried blood and torn scraps of flesh, mailed to her by the Gestapo after her husband's death. In his *Autobiography* Muir wrote of the men he saw in the photograph:

> They all seemed to be in their late twenties, and it suddenly came into my mind that they had been bred by the first world war. . . . [Our friend] pointed at one young man and said without expression: that is the one who strangled my husband. But it might have

been any of the others. They stared out from the photograph with the confidence of the worthless who find power left in their hands like a tip hastily dropped by a frightened world.[7]

Muir's poem about the photograph is a first-person dramatization of the sort of mentality he ascribes to Regan, Goneril, and Edmund in his essay on *King Lear* (from a 1946 lecture), that mentality which sees "things in a continuous present divested of all associations, denuded of memory and the depth which memory gives to life, . . . claim[ing] a liberty which is proper to nature but not to society."[8] "The Usurpers" depicts how casual the speakers are about dismissing traditional knowledge: "It was not hard to still the ancestral voices: / A careless thought, less than a thought could do it."

This perspective, invaluable to the empirical methods of pure and applied science, which are based on systematic suppression of qualitative experience, devastates human life, which thrives on imagination, stories, and values that can be felt or intuited but not measured. The Gestapo men, like the power-obsessed characters in *King Lear*, boast of a

> liberty
> No one has known before, nor could have borne,
> For it is rooted in this deepening silence
> That is our work and has become our kingdom.

Dissociated from a culture that conveys a sense of meaning and relatedness, the speakers mistakenly believe that this alienation constitutes genuine liberty: "We dare do all we think, / Since there's no one to check us, here or elsewhere." And the end of the poem implies that the speakers' naturalistic bias leads, ironically, to a cold objectification of nature: "It is a lie that they are witnesses, / That the mountains judge us, brooks tell tales about us. . . . These are imaginations. We are free."

The last line is especially telling: "freedom" in this sense requires the contemptuous or defensive dismissal by reason of all so-called superstitions of the past. Another of Muir's poems from *One Foot in Eden*, "The Cloud," satirizes political systems based on this attitude. It was written during Muir's last year in Prague, shortly after the Soviet takeover. The communists—although their impersonality, said Muir, was not as cruel as that of the Nazis—were able to impose their system only by carefully censoring

---

7. Muir, *Autobiography*, 267.

8. Muir, *The Politics of King Lear*, 17. This essay was reprinted in the 1965 edition of *Essays on Literature and Society*,

all spontaneity of personal relationship and feeling, a ploy Muir experienced firsthand when two government officials attended and took notes on his lectures at the university. For Muir, as he wrote in his *Autobiography*, the communists, like the Nazis, "called up a vast image of impersonal power, the fearful shape of our modern inhumanity":

> Their categories, the working class, the capitalists, the bourgeoisie, the communists, the anti-communists, were far more real to them than . . . human beings. Their moral judgments were judgments of their categories. . . . They could understand a good worker, but a good human being was an abstraction which fell outside their sphere of thought.[9]

One day Muir and his wife were driving to a writers' retreat at Dobris Castle near Prague, when they rounded a corner and saw in a field "A young man harrowing, hidden in dust; he seemed / A prisoner walking in a moving cloud / Made by himself for his own purposes." Muir, of course, knew nothing of this man's actual political convictions. The lines are a satirical description of the worker that communist ideology supposedly defended. Muir is applying the anti-imaginative constructs of communism to one of its own, to show how it failed to provide the liberation of spirit it promised.

> And there he grew and was as if exalted
> To more than man, yet not, not glorified:
> A pillar of dust moving in dust; no more.
> . . .
> We looked and wondered; the dry cloud moved on
> With its interior image.

The Muirs continued on to the writers' center, where they heard a talk by a "preacher from Urania," who praised "the good dust, man's ultimate salvation." Communist ideology, Muir suggests, condemned the very person it claimed to free; it limited him to an identity entirely circumscribed by "the biological sequence," so that he could imagine himself only as "a blindfold mask on a pillar of dust."

Both "The Usurpers" and "The Cloud" are typical of the sort of political poetry Muir wrote: the subjects are universalized; the images and ideas, with few exceptions, could apply as easily to any place or time with similar circumstances. Muir almost always looked for the essentials behind and beneath surface conditions; his poems show us that politics, societies, and

---

9. Muir, *Autobiography*, 277.

history are "fables" as well as literal "stories." (The early version of Muir's *Autobiography* was called *The Story and the Fable* because he wanted to tell not only his life's events, but their context in the larger picture of things.) In Muir's political poetry, history is reimagined as an internal event. Muir depicted our time as one of transition, an *interregnum* of civilization, during which the danger is great that we can forget altogether the meanings and associations that make specifically *human* life possible. His personal struggle to assimilate (for he never really adapted to it) this hypertechnological epoch resulted in some of the most singular writing of his time, immensely useful to those of us who, even if we have never known any other way of life, are trying to understand, articulate, and address the inadequacies of the modern world. Obviously, to move forward we can't be merely sentimental or nostalgic about what we've lost or abandoned; but it is equally true that forgetting it limits us to our own myopic and dystopian creation. Muir's poetry and prose are there to help us remember.

GIUSEPPE UNGARETTI
AND THE IMAGE OF DESOLATION

✳

P UBLISHED RIGHT AFTER WORLD War I, Giuseppe Ungaretti's first collection, *Allegria di naufragi* (Joy of Shipwrecks; 1919), was a milestone of modern poetry in Italy and established him overnight as one of the leading poets of his generation.[1] Ungaretti's poetry was as new, strange, and, for many Italian readers, exciting as Eliot's *Prufrock* or Pound's *Mauberley* were to American and English readers of that period. As Eugenio Montale would say years later, the innovators of modernist poetry in Italy set out to "wring the neck of the old aulic eloquence"—namely, and immediately before them, the romanticism of Giosuè Carducci, the sentimentality of Giovanni Pascoli, and the bombast of Gabriele D'Annunzio. At the start of the 1910s, the Crepuscular poets—most famously, Corrado Govoni, Sergio Corazzini, Guido Gozzano, and Marino Moretti—came out with their Jules Laforgue–influenced, ironic, subdued style, consciously breaking with the past augustness of the formidable Italian poetic tradition. Their vocabulary and syntax were those of everyday speech and their tone was self-effacing. The landscapes in their poetry were no longer the grandiose ones of Carducci or D'Annunzio, but rather, enclosed gardens and other domesticated spaces. Gozzano introduced modern neologisms into his poems: *fotografia*, *dagherròtipo*, and so on, as well as foreign words. The meter and rhyme schemes of the Crepusculars were less regular than

---

1. This essay is the introduction to my volume of translations from Ungaretti, *Selected Poems*, somewhat revised for the present context. Ungaretti's poems that I quote here are taken from that edition as well.

Italian poets formerly had used, and so their work was an important stage in the move toward *vers libre* in Italy.

An even more radical aesthetic, and one that Ungaretti also emulated in his early writing, was launched by Filippo Marinetti's Futurist manifesto, which was published in 1912 in *Le Figaro* in Paris. The aspect of Marinetti's monomaniacal rant that had a special relevance for Ungaretti was his proposal of a new poetic language of *parole en liberté*, joined in ever deeper analogical associations. Nineteen-twelve was the very year Ungaretti came to Paris, at age twenty-four, from his native city of Alexandria—interestingly, also Marinetti's hometown (although they didn't know each other there). French culture and education had been fashionable in Alexandria ever since Napoleon occupied the city, so Ungaretti was bilingual from the start. His early immersion in authors such as Baudelaire, Rimbaud, Laforgue, and Mallarmé, rather than the more usual fare for Italian poets at that time, had everything to do with Ungaretti's decisive, innovative influence on Italian letters. Ungaretti came to Europe equipped for radical change. He immediately became an integral part of the intense creative ferment that was under way in Europe just before the war, as if in anticipation of the irreparable destruction that the war would inflict. As Ungaretti's close friend the Futurist Ardengo Soffici put it, the arts were breaking with conventional forms in order to draw closer to the fluidity of life, to its impressions.

Ungaretti was in Paris for less than two years, but that was long enough for him to refer to that time, more than fifty years later, as his cultural and social coming-of-age. He attended Henri Bergson's and other lectures at the Sorbonne, became a close friend of Apollinaire, and came into regular contact with the major exponents of the avant-garde: Picasso, Georges Braque, Fernand Léger, Giorgio De Chirico, Max Jacob, and others. Having become friendly with the Futurists Giovanni Papini, Aldo Palazzeschi, and Soffici, he was invited to collaborate with them on their new journal, *Lacerba*, where Ungaretti first published his poems. *Lacerba*, edited in Milan, and *La Voce*, in Florence, were the main organs for the earliest stages of Italian modernism.

As always, although Ungaretti was in the thick of cultural activity and public discussion of it, he went his own way. Like many of the most talented modernists, he was as much at odds with the avant-garde as he was a part of it. He was iconoclastic only to the extent that cultural detritus and insincere formalism were in the way of reality. The essence of language, the deep resonance of the authentic poetic line, could be rediscovered only by starting over again with its basic units: the syllable, word, or phrase. Ungaretti was separated from his Futurist and Crepuscular peers by his moral seriousness and philosophical fervor: "While I did not use the word except when it came to me infused with moral content," he wrote, "they . . . asked nothing of the word but a physical impressionability."[2] Another way of saying this is that Ungaretti remained a committed humanist, as demonstrated, for instance, by his apprenticeship to Petrarch and Leopardi. He always defended human culture, even as he acknowledged its transience. For Ungaretti, cultural forms, though always in need of renewal, are all there is at times between us and a terrifying emptiness. Such a humanistic stance would put Ungaretti at odds with the French Surrealists and with Freudian reductionism. Ungaretti would always espouse, as he put it, a waking dream, *un sogno ad occhi aperti*, rather than the somnambulism of the Surrealists. In an essay on Paul Valéry he wrote: "Valéry learns from Poe that in order to understand the genesis of a work of art one must start, not with an initial emotion, but from the technical means put to work by the artist to produce such and such an effect." For Ungaretti, this classical perspective would always be a safeguard against solipsism and aesthetic decadence. His summary statement about Valéry could also be said of him: "to extreme turbulence he opposed . . . extreme precision."[3]

Just after Italy's entry into World War I in 1915, Ungaretti (who had already enlisted in the army) was sent to the Carso, in northern Italy, scene of some of the war's bloodiest battles. The immediate crisis of the war, of witnessing and being so close to death day after day, was the alembic in which Ungaretti's developing sensibility was purified. Not only did he lack the time to second-guess the phrases that he jotted down as they came into his head, but he had every reason to believe that no one would ever read them. He was no more likely to survive the almost daily battles on the Austrian front than was the friend he wrote about in "Vigil":

> An entire night
> thrown down
> beside a
> butchered
> companion with his
> grimacing
> mouth turned

2. Ungaretti, "Punto di mira," in *Saggi e interventi*, 298. All translations are mine.

3. Ungaretti, "Discorso per Valéry," in *Saggi e interventi*, 629–30.

> to the full moon
> with his congested hands
> thrust
> into my silence
> I wrote
> letters full of love
>
> I have never held
> so hard
> to life

Or, as Ungaretti said, the war suddenly revealed to him the language of his own voice as a poet, because he only had a few moments to jot down his words, which were therefore all the more intense and charged with meaning. A striking quality of Ungaretti's war poems is the sense that the person who speaks them is transparent or egoless:

> When I find
> a word
> in this my silence
> it is dug into my life
> like an abyss ("Envoi")

Or:

> I waver
> at the corner of a road
> like a firefly ("June")

To say nothing of his famous minimalist gem "Mattina" (Morning): "M'illumino / d'immenso," which translates literally as "I am luminous with immensity" but says much more in the compact form of its original language. When Ungaretti refers to himself as "Ungaretti, man of pain," *uomo di pena*, the directness moves us not because of one individual's suffering, but because an ordinary soldier's oblique identification with Christ, the universal man, consecrates the suffering and death that war inflicts.

As a student of Bergson, Ungaretti had received philosophical justification for his natural penchant for a knowledge that is global and immediate, intuitive, reaching into the essences of things by sympathy. As Glauco Cambon put it in his book-length essay on Ungaretti, "The basic conception underlying Ungaretti's poetry is that of the existence of a universal, cosmic life to which man is integrally joined in a nonrational, intuitive way."[4] Ungaretti, like many leading modernist poets, had a quasi-religious notion of his poetic calling: he wanted to "free the word from its conventional superstructures so that it might regain its original pristine form," as Ungaretti said, so that it might "penetrate into one's darkest recess, without disturbing or being able to uncover its secret."[5] Hence the distinction Ungaretti liked to make, following Leopardi, between the two Italian words for "word"—*parola* and *vocabolo*—the latter referring to literal meanings, the former to a word's ineffable essence. Ungaretti was explicit about his metaphysical conception of poetry: "It is the search to establish a relationship with the inviolable secret within the divine creatrix." In his comments on his late poem "Canzone," Ungaretti said that the moments the poet can be a poet are exactly those when the "primal image" "ruptures the ice" of habitual daily consciousness.[6] And around the same time he noted that his early war poems were an attempt to close the gap between language and what he most needed to say. "Such a poetry," as scholar Giusy Oddo puts it, "annuls the distance between word and object, between word and image, its sense being captured in a spark of intuition."[7] A literary label for this aesthetic is Hermeticism (actually coined in 1936 by Francesco Flora, a critic who considered Ungaretti's elliptical style too mannered). Hermetic poetry was a poetry that sought not to describe or represent, but to evoke. Some of the Italian poets, besides Ungaretti, who are considered hermetic are Montale, Salvatore Quasimodo, Alfonso Gatto, and Leonardo Sinisgalli. The Hermeticists were never a "school" as such; they were simply some poets who shared, in their different ways, an aspiration toward "pure poetry."

AFTER UNGARETTI LEFT ALEXANDRIA and started to discover his ancestral roots in Italy and his cultural and intellectual roots in Paris, there would be no turning back: he would remain, as he put it, a man with many homelands. It could be said that Italy for him was the land of the fathers—his own paternity and Italy's poetic patrimony—while Alexandria was maternal, less linked in his imagination to the masculine creators of culture than to the enveloping maternal world of sustaining imagination and unfathomable mystery.

4. Cambon, *Giuseppe Ungaretti*, 5.

5. Ungaretti on his poem "Commiato," in *Tutte le poesie*, 524–25.

6. Ungaretti, *Tutte le poesie*, 552–53.

7. Oddo, *Ungaretti*, 2.

> In a bay in Alexandria there was discovered . . . , sunken in water, an ancient port, the primitive port of Alexandria: a buried port, that is. . . . The reason why this port has become the symbol of my poetry is easy to explain. There is a secret in us that the poet dives into, and reaching the port he discovers this secret, and so can pass on that little bit of consolation which a man can give to the soul.[8]

If the poems in *L'allegria* represented found objects retrieved from the maternal buried harbor, those of *Sentimento del tempo* (A Sense of Time; 1936), his second complete collection, gave form to the beginning of his long experiment with the reassimilation of the Italian poetic tradition. Ungaretti's impulse was part of a general need for reconstruction after the war. What this meant for literature was represented by Vincenzo Cardarelli's founding of *La Ronda* in 1919 in Rome, the express purpose of which was to promote a new classical style, "to reconnect [said *La Ronda*'s manifesto] to the greatest and most authentic Italian tradition, [which was] interrupted after Leopardi and Manzoni."[9] For Ungaretti, then, the naked flashes of insight that characterized the poems of his first book needed to be filled out and grounded by the memory of history. *Sentimento del tempo*, as its title states, was a return to the temporal dimension after the split-second flashes of the war poems. In a piece he wrote in 1930 for Turin's *Gazzetta del Popolo* he described how after the war he set to work on assimilating the Italian poets—Jacopone da Todi, Cavalcanti, Dante, Petrarch, Tasso, Leopardi, and others—not, he said, for literary research: "I was looking for the song in them . . . the song of the Italian language." And: "It was my heartbeat that I wanted to feel in harmony with the heartbeat of my betters from a passionately loved land."[10]

Ungaretti's attachment to Italy and his Italian roots also led him to adhere to Mussolini, shortly after meeting him, when Mussolini was a leading socialist agitator and journalist, just before Italy entered the First World War. Ungaretti's belief in fascism lasted for many years, although he did eventually renounce it and was critical of some of its policies. The scholar Luciano Rebay has charted the progress and nature of Ungaretti's politics during this period by following letters exchanged by Ungaretti with his friend Jean Paulhan, who from 1925 to 1940 was the editor of the

---

8. Ungaretti, "Ungaretti commenta Ungaretti," in *Saggi e interventi*, 817.

9. Quoted in Baldini and Cecchi, *Carteggio: 1911–1959*, 173.

10. Quoting himself in "Ragioni di una poesia" (1949), in *Saggi e interventi*, 751–52.

literary journal *La Nouvelle Revue Française*.[11] What comes out of Rebay's analysis is this: while Ungaretti believed in Mussolini "without a shadow of a doubt," the basis of Ungaretti's position was his view of Italian fascism as a movement for gaining rights for exploited Italian workers, restoring order and self-respect to a badly fragmented postwar Italy, and preserving tradition in industrialized Italian society. At no point in Ungaretti's letters or other writings do we see the racism and imperialist power mania that Italian fascism increasingly represented and that eventually led to Mussolini's downfall. Ungaretti was patriotic, but he was too cosmopolitan and tolerant to be narrowly nationalistic. He was vocal about his opposition to racist laws—he got into some political trouble for this at one point—and his anger over social conditions was directed toward the wide gap between rich and poor in early-twentieth-century Italy. Rebay shows that Ungaretti believed passionately in a political system that would be "for the people" and thought fascism was the system that could best accomplish this, bringing about a social order capable of guaranteeing dignified work for all in accordance with their aptitudes and talents, regardless of class. In other words, Ungaretti's *mussolinismo* was based on the years leading up to the March on Rome, in which Mussolini's main agenda was a populist and antibourgeois revolution. Clearly, Ungaretti came to this view as the working-class son of emigrants from Tuscany. A high proportion of Italian writers (95 percent, according to the notes section in the Mondadori edition of Ungaretti's collected essays) were attracted by Mussolini's "pararevolutionary, paraprogressive, antibourgeois" promises of social change, while at the same time Mussolini's achievements, his public works and so on, were widely admired in Europe and America.[12] This was the context in which Ungaretti's publisher solicited a preface from Mussolini for the 1923 edition of *Il porto sepolto* (The Buried Harbor). The idealism of Ungaretti and many other Italian writers, not balanced by facing and/or knowing the dark side of Mussolini's career, resembled that of the well-meaning but grossly mistaken modernist artists and intellectuals who were attracted by communist revolutions that turned out to be tyrannies.

Ungaretti's aim as a poet, meanwhile, was to find a modern idiom, cadence, and meter for bringing together the present with *un antico strumento musicale*, thereby linking modern poetry with the Italian patrimony. Ungaretti turned especially to Petrarch, Tasso, and Leopardi for models

11. See Rebay, "Jean Paulhan–Giuseppe Ungaretti."

12. Ungaretti, *Saggi e interventi*, 909.

of the Italian hendecasyllabic line—the Italian equivalent of iambic pentameter in English—which he called "the natural poetic measure of Italian speech" in a 1927 article.[13] Thus we find, in *Sentimento*, in addition to the blunt, concrete diction of *L'allegria*, a modernist grandiloquence: broken syntactical units have been transformed into a more fluid, complex organization; instead of the first-person speaker in the present tense, there is an evocative use of the past tense; and staccato phrasing has become mellifluous speech. As if to announce the decisive change in style, Ungaretti opens his book with these beautiful lines:

> Dall'ampia ansia dell'alba
> Svelata alberatura.

> Out of daybreak's huge and restless hunger
> Trees—like masts—revealed. ("O Night")

It is no wonder that in the 1930s Ungaretti became one of the most admired writers in Europe: the poems in *Sentimento* are so richly textured and perfectly made, the emotion in them so focused and intense.

The 1920s and early 1930s were happy years for him. He and his wife lived in Marino, one of the *castelli romani*, the ancient hilltowns east of Rome, where, as Ungaretti said, the feel of a small Renaissance town in the country was still intact. They had children, a son and a daughter, and Ungaretti rediscovered his ancestral soul in the pastoral landscape. The classical deities were realities now.

> He landed on a waterfront where evening
> Was everlasting, thick with ancient spellbound trees,
> And made his way in,
> And a flutter of feathers
> Loosened from the piercing palpitations
> Of the scalding water
> Called him back, and he thought he saw
> (Fading, reflourishing)
> A shade; climbing again,
> He saw it was a nymph
> Asleep on her feet, her arms around an elm. ("The Island")

In other poems, this glimpse of sensual innocence was associated with the childhood world of Africa:

---

13. Ungaretti, "Difesa dell'endecasillabo," in *Saggi e interventi*, 158.

No more now will I go off alone
Between the vast plain and the open sea,
Nor hear, from far-off ages, homely, clear,
Loosening in the limpid air, shrill sounds;
Nor will crazy fantasy go stripping nude
The acid graces,
Exalting them in fabled forms;
Nor will I pursue Diana
Stepping from the sparse palm grove
In a fleet gown of light . . . ("Memory of Africa")

There is an opalesque, polysemous effect in this strange and wonderful poem that I have tried to carry over in my translation. For Ungaretti does not merely draw on memory, personal and collective; he attempts to reproduce its effects, as if the poem itself were an *experience* of memory.

Another way Ungaretti revived traditional forms during the 1920s was in his return to Catholicism. During Holy Week in 1928 he went on retreat at the monastery of Subiaco, where he renewed his commitment to his childhood faith and started working on the longest poem in *Sentimento*, "La pietà" (Mercy), an Ecclesiastes-like proclamation about the relative futility of all human endeavor, including writing poetry:

I have peopled the silence with names.

Have I ripped mind and heart to pieces
To fall into servitude to words?

I am the king of phantoms.

O dry leaves,
Soul carried here and there . . .

In the second half of *Sentimento* he substitutes the naked nymphs of the African oasis and the woods of Marino with a search for meaning and moral depth. The Bible, not classical mythology, is now his text, notes Glauco Cambon.

What difference does sin make
If it no longer leads to purity?

The flesh can scarcely recollect
A time when it was strong.

The soul is used and foolish.

God, consider our frailty. ("Mercy")

Once *Sentimento* was written, the trajectory of Ungaretti's writing life was set. One of the last poems he wrote for the collection, "Auguri per il proprio compleanno" (Greetings for His Own Birthday), reiterates the themes of lost youth and disillusioned aspiration. Just after Ungaretti wrote this poem, in 1935, he conceived the idea for *La terra promessa* (The Promised Land; 1950), his fourth collection, which explores these motifs in depth. Joseph Cary, in his 1993 study of Montale, Ungaretti, and Umberto Saba, *Three Modern Italian Poets*, rightly criticizes *Terra promessa* for being too mannered and overly concerned with literary precedent. Ungaretti had flirted with drying himself out on abstraction and iconoclasm, and had lost some of his spark. He was far too much of a poet to succeed, however, and so there are some very beautiful rarefactions in *Terra promessa*:

> That negligible bit of sand which slides
> Without a sound and settles in the hourglass,
> And the fleeting impressions on the fleshy-pink,
> The perishable fleshy-pink, of a cloud . . . ("Variations on Nothing")

For me, the poems of *Terra promessa* are like exquisite alpine flora atop an ascetic crag. "Canzone," for example, probably Ungaretti's most hermetic poem, depicts in time-lapse detail the changeover from night to dawn. Ungaretti's 1964 explication of this poem demonstrates how precise its images are. When he refers to the sunrise "Enervating into rainbow echoes," for instance, the physical reality represented in the poem corresponds to how "we know reality only through echoes," and that "sunrise doesn't reveal a pure world, but a world that documents its own ruin."[14] I was struck, when I first read this passage, by the implied reference to Ungaretti's experience in the war, documented in "Vanità" (Vanity), an early poem about watching the sun rise over the aftermath of a battlefield:

> Suddenly
> the lucid
> awesome
> vastness
> is high
> above the rubble

14. Ungaretti, *Saggi e interventi*, 552.

And the man
bent
over the sun-
shocked
water
finds
he's a shadow

Rocked and
gently
broken

Ungaretti's focus changed for several years between the time he conceived of *Terra promessa* and the time he actually wrote it. In 1936 he was offered the chair of Italian literature and language at the University of São Paulo. He and his family moved Brazil, and just as Ungaretti was getting used to his new prestige, his world fell apart: first, the death of his nine-year-old son from complications associated with appendicitis; then the death of his brother and, toward the end of his stay in São Paolo (he was hired to a professorship at the University of Rome in 1942, a position he would hold until his retirement), the outbreak of World War II and the occupation of Rome. The death of Antonietto, his son, stirred such desperate emotion that the resulting poetry was more violent and visceral than anything since the war poems, although combined now with the artfulness that Ungaretti had acquired:

> The many, gigantic, jumbled, glaucous stones
> Shuddering still within the hidden slings
> Of suffocated elemental flames
> Or in the terrible virgin torrents'
> Headlong unappeasable caress—
> Above the dazzling glare of sand, relentless
> Along an empty horizon, remember? ("You Were Broken")

The Brazilian wilderness provided images for nature in its unrelentingly merciless aspect. This is very different from the poems in *L'allegria*, where the elements are usually portrayed as healing and restorative. The change of perspective makes sense: the war was caused by human beings, while Antonietto's death was a result of natural causes. As in Leopardi's famous poem "To Silvia," which was a model for Ungaretti's poem "Tu ti spezzasti" (You Were Broken), nature is blamed for plundering innocence:

Happy grace,
You were not able not to break
Against a blindness so implacable
You simple breath and crystal,

Too human flash of light for the pitiless,
Savage, unrelenting, droning
Roar of a naked sun.

A striking aspect of Ungaretti's work as a whole is that he so consistently, powerfully, and honestly writes about death. *Il dolore* (Affliction; 1947), where the above poem was published, is the collection in which Ungaretti most vividly combines personal grief with collective suffering. One part of the collection, "Roma occupata," confronts the reality of Rome under occupation during World War II: a cradle of western civilization in the throes of violence and chaos. Ungaretti despairs over the breakdown of culture and humanitarian values, but ultimately affirms the power of creative human endeavor to survive the darker forces that always threaten it.

May your sudden pinkish trace,
Mother mind, ascend again,
And return to amaze me;
Come back to life, unhoped for,
Measure inconceivable, peace;

Make it so I, in the balanced landscape,
May mouth again the sounds of artless speech. ("In Veins")

Ungaretti's reading and translating of Góngora and Racine—in addition to his interpretation of Michelangelo and the Roman baroque—had given him models for a refined but robust art that is haunted by a sense of emptiness and entropy.

MUCH HAS BEEN SAID about the connection between Ungaretti's search for geographical belonging and his "quest for essentialness" (as Cambon put it) in his poetry.[15] Ungaretti's early poem about his Arab friend's suicide in Paris suggests that he could see himself in Mohammed Sceab's despair over having been uprooted:

15. Cambon, *Giuseppe Ungaretti*, 8.

21

. . . [he] no longer knew
how to live
in his people's tent
where you hear the Koran
being chanted
while you savor your coffee

And he didn't know how
to set free
the song
of his desolation ("In Memory Of")

Ungaretti's parents and ancestors were from Lucca, in Tuscany. His father had been drawn to Alexandria by Ismail Pasha's government's demand for foreigners to come and labor in public works projects like the Suez Canal. Ungaretti's father died from an illness contracted while at work on excavations in the canal when Giuseppe was two years old. His mother raised him and his older brother with her earnings from the bakery she owned in an Italian section of Alexandria. Alexandria and the desert next to which Ungaretti lived, as well as the Bedouin culture he witnessed there, became huge, timeless images in the poet's imagination. For Ungaretti, the desert was the fittest of images for the eternity in which our lives are the mirages. He was ambivalent about the desert and the city that borders it. At times they are places of Edenic bliss:

Now
the clear sky
is closed
like the jasmine
at this hour
in my native Africa ("June")

At other times they are places of delusion and madness:

If the Arab returns from the desert, ah! mastiffs are barking in his veins. This is why the nomad is incurable: the desert is a wine, and it is a drug, and it sets a rage on fire that can be quenched only in blood and in languorous loves.

Out of the many senses of death that his thousands-of-years existence has impressed in his veins, the Egyptian has received the saddest sense from the Arab: that the desire for pleasure is a radical thirst, suffering that does not let up except in madness. This sense: that madness is like an increase of soul, that the soul's prize is liberation into the mortal pleasure of the senses. ("The Laugh of the Djinn Rull")[16]

As Ungaretti said in a 1965 interview with Ferdinando Camon: "The image of desolation has been an obsession for me since my first poems. To be precise, the desert was in me: from it was born . . . the motion and the feeling of infinity, of the primordial, of the decline into nothingness."[17] Thus the desert represented for him both the fullness and the emptiness of eternity; and Alexandria, the city on the desert, was a symbol for the ephemerality of civilization itself. The austerity of Ungaretti's spiritual- ity—his negative theology—had much in common with that of the Desert Fathers, the ancient monks in the desert near Alexandria. Ungaretti was strongly attracted to Platonism (as was Bergson), but he was also a skep- tic. In contrast to Blake, whom he admired and translated, and in contrast to Dante as well, Ungaretti did not ultimately trust that products of the imagination were anything other than mirages. Hence his obsession with the baroque and its "multiplication of units" to fill in "the void," the fear of emptiness which, he believed, motivated the busyness of the baroque style. As he put it in his introductory essay to *Sentimento del tempo*:

> When one is in the presence of the Colosseum, an enormous cylinder with empty eye sockets, one has the sense of emptiness. Naturally, having the sense of emptiness, one cannot help but also have the dread of emptiness. Those things piled up, coming from every direction, so that not a bit of space is left, of free space, everything is filled, nothing is left, nothing freed. That dread of emptiness, one can feel it in Rome infinitely more than in any other place on earth, more even than in the desert. I believe that from the dread of emptiness issues, not the need of filling that space with it-matters-not-what thing, but all the drama of the art of Michelangelo.
>
> When I said that the Baroque provoked the sense of empti- ness, that the aesthetic of the Roman Baroque had been initiated by the dread of emptiness, I mentioned the Colosseum. I'm afraid I haven't been clear enough. The dread in the Baroque originated with the intolerable idea of a body without a soul. A skeleton evokes the dread of emptiness.[18]

16. Ungaretti, *Selected Poems*, 158–59.
17. Ungaretti, *Saggi e interventi*, 836.
18. Ungaretti, *Selected Poems*, 271.

For Ungaretti, poetry is a means for using memory, the collective memory of language, to rediscover innocence, the world resurrected in its primordial purity. A challenge in Ungaretti's time and ours is to reinterpret the present in relation to a disintegrated past. Ungaretti rejected the Futurists' pretense that the rubble of the past could simply be swept aside, while also affirming Leopardi's despairing realization that an age was spent. As Ungaretti wrote in an essay four years before his death in 1970:

> After the war we witnessed a change in the world that separated us from what we used to be and from what we once had made and done, as if at one blow millions of years had passed. Things grew old, fit only for a museum. Today everything that is stored in books is listened to as a testimony of the past, not as our own mode of expression. . . . Something in the world of languages is totally finished. . . . We are men cut off from our own depths.

Modern (or postmodern) humanity, he said, is "trapped in the impossibility of speech, in a violence stronger than the word."[19] It is remarkable that Ungaretti, like his master Leopardi, expressed such torment so exquisitely.

19. Ungaretti, "Delle parole estranee e del sogno d'un universo di Michaux e forse anche mio," in *Saggi e interventi*, 842–43.

Cold Dawn

Yeats, the Gyres, and Poetic Style

S OME ARTISTS ARE BOTH of their time and outside or beyond it. For example, Dante is a poet of his medieval culture but he also prefigures the Renaissance and has been considered the first modern poet. Michelangelo's style evolves from early Renaissance classicism into his later mannerist phase, anticipating the baroque. Beethoven's astonishing inventiveness bridges the classical period and the romantic, and is even, in his late quartets, hauntingly modern. W. B. Yeats's early work draws on the Pre-Raphaelite movement, with the prose influence of Walter Pater, but his style gradually emerges from that nostalgic dreaminess. He goes on to become a poet of kinetic and vigorous language, shunning easy mellifluousness in his search for a beauty (as he puts it in his 1914 poems "The Dawn" and "The Fisherman") as cold, passionate, and wanton as the dawn. During World War I, the arch-modernist Ezra Pound edited Yeats's style out of its early romanticism into its later, bracing modernity. At the same time, while Yeats surely did become a "modern" poet, whatever that may mean, he was not modern in the same way that Pound and Eliot were, let alone in the manner of Auden or Larkin. Yeats's writings, finally, are sui generis, like the work of certain other visionary artists who have worked at the peak level of their craft. Yeats's later writings were modern but also something more—universal, and expressing an inchoate civilizational shift.

In this essay, I consider how the evolution of Yeats's poetic style throughout his remarkable career navigated the inexorable flux of the modern era. First, I will describe Yeats's characterization of these world-transforming changes in terms of his theory of the gyres. Then, I will discuss his notion of the Unity of Being, or spiritual wholeness, as a core aspiration in an age of shifting points of reference and fragmented traditions, which he felt keenly as a religiously sensitive man who nevertheless could not find fulfillment in his native religion, Christianity. Lastly I will portray his stylistic changes as expressions of his search for Unity of Being. The connection between realism and the modern age is well known. Going back to its roots in the Renaissance, modernism in the West brought a return to pre-Christian worldliness, in the positive as well as the negative senses, which countless artists and writers have articulated in their work. A representative dictum of twentieth-century poetry was William Carlos Williams's "no ideas but in things." Yeats, however, was rare in that he applied his increasingly direct and earthy style to making archetypal or metaphysical subject matter tangible and concrete. He was a realist in terms of his language and engagement with the world, but he never lost sight, as he puts it in his early poem "To Ireland in the Coming Times," of "things discovered in the deep / Where only body's laid asleep."[1]

Yeats had much to say, of course, about the great upheavals of our epoch, or what he called the reversal of the gyres. His thoughts on this are most explicitly laid out in A Vision, which organizes and elaborates material communicated through his wife's automatic-writing mediumship shortly after their marriage, when Yeats was in his early fifties. The fundamental symbol in this system is the double gyre, two interlocking and gyrating cones, with the point of each turning into the center of the base of the other. One gyre moves progressively wider in a spiral, and once that gyre arrives at its point of maximum expansion it then begins to narrow until it reaches its end-point, which is also the origin of the new gyre. So as one increases, the other decreases. The alternating cones represent opposing principles whose synthesis and antithesis manifest in the dynamics of human personality and collective historical cycles.

In Yeats's understanding, drawing on his hermetic and magical research, the outer world and the inner world are reciprocal or complementary—so that, for instance, fairy lambs in Irish lore are born in November rather than the spring. As the gyre of the soul expands, the gyre of outer life contracts; or in Heraclitus's terms that Yeats liked to quote, gods and men are always dying each other's life and living each other's death. In Plato's Phaedrus, which is one of the inspirations for A Vision, the soul's chariot is

---

1. Quotations from Yeats's poems are from the Macmillan edition of Collected Poems.

pulled by both the horse of instinct and the horse of spiritual aspiration, a dynamic that generates tension and conflict in the human soul. Yeats called the two phases delineated by the interaction of the gyres the subjective or antithetical tincture (or phase) and the objective or primary tincture. As he describes them in *A Vision*: "The *primary* is that which serves, the *antithetical* is that which creates."[2] We note the dualism in this system, a polarity of energies, including a yin-yang sexual polarity, which together form a whole. Indeed, the tension of opposites pervades Yeats's work from start to finish and accounts for much of its dynamism and force.

In *A Vision* Yeats describes how the alternation of primary and antithetical phases results in varying combinations which manifest in the human personality. There are twenty-six basic personality types plotted in terms of a lunar month, with the new moon (phase 1) and the full moon (phase 15) left out because for human beings purely objective or subjective personality is impossible, since everything in earthly life is a mixture of some kind. Predominantly subjective or antithetical individuals, such as Blake (in phase 16) and Yeats himself and Dante (in phase 17), are driven to create, pursuing an image of themselves that contrasts with their empirical self, which Yeats refers to as the Will. The contrasting image is what Yeats calls the Mask, articulated succinctly in his 1915 poem "Ego Dominus Tuus": "I call to my own opposite, summon all / That I have handled least, least looked upon"; or as he puts it in his prose work *Per Amica Silentia Lunae*, which opens with that poem: "All happiness depends on the energy to assume the mask of some other life, on a re-birth as something not one's self, something created in a moment and perpetually renewed."[3] On the other hand, all predominantly objective people must flee from the Mask, and wake from dreams to live and elaborate reality as it is. An example is an artist such as Rembrandt (in phase 23), who finds beauty in the commonplace or even in what is considered ugly. An individual in an objective or primary phase has the task of self-effacement in relation to the objective world, while an individual in a subjective phase seeks self-realization. This forging or glorification of the self is fundamental in Yeats, and underlies his attraction to Nietzsche, to the pre-Christian image of a hero such as Cuchulain, and, later and more profoundly, to the teachings of Hindu Vedānta, where the universal Self is the transcendent and permanent principle of the individual self. From one incarnation to the next, says Yeats, the soul picks

2. Yeats, *A Vision*, 85.

3. Originally published in 1918; cited from Yeats, *Mythologies*, 334.

up where it left off in the Great Wheel, until, after twenty-eight deaths and rebirths, it has experienced the whole gamut and returns to the starting point.

The same system of the Great Wheel is applied also to historical cycles. Subjective and objective eras alternate, and every two thousand years an era is inaugurated by the birth of a god. So the Christian era has been objective—the self striving to escape from personality, emphasizing virtues such as obedience, pity, chastity, forgiveness, self-negation. Before the Christian era was the subjective Greek age, whose ideal virtues were beauty, aristocracy, sexual power, heroic splendor. The Christian era began with a virgin birth, while the classical era began with the rape of Leda by Zeus in the shape of a swan (recounted by Yeats in his sonnet "Leda and the Swan"), a union that led to the birth of Helen and Clytemnestra and the subsequent epoch-making events of the Trojan War. Yeats's system predicted the subjective age supplanting the objective one of Christian virtue in about the year 2000, when the rough beast would be "slouching towards Bethlehem," as he puts it in his famous poem of 1919 "The Second Coming."

The double spiral of Yeats's gyres, with their complementary motions, parallels Blake's poem "The Mental Traveller."[4] This dense symbolic narrative describes a cycle in which two figures, one male and one female, grow from infancy to old age and back to infancy again. Each grows younger as the other grows older, so that one is oldest when the other is being born. The male baby, having grown to manhood and broken his manacles, binds the woman who has grown ever younger. As the man becomes old he wanders away, and his place is taken by "a little Female Babe," who then grows up, pursued by the reborn male principle, until she ages and becomes "a Woman old." Yeats wrote that "the woman and the man [in Blake's poem] are two competing gyres growing at one another's expense"[5]—in other words, they are a figurative enactment of the cyclical myth that Yeats lays out in A Vision. The ultimate source for both Blake and Yeats is Plato's dialogue The Statesman, where Plato says that the Divinity conducts the universe to a certain point and then releases it like a spring which unwinds to its contrary. The coiled spring of Plato is echoed by Yeats's gyres. Plato describes a Great Year of the alternation between the golden race, which is born directly from the earth and is mindful of God, and the fallen race,

4. See Kathleen Raine, "From Blake to A Vision," in Yeats the Initiate, 106–76.

5. Quoted in Raine, "From Blake to A Vision," 154, from Yeats's first edition of A Vision, 134.

which is begotten from one another and is forgetful of God. In the golden age of Kronos when heaven is dominant, humanity progresses from age to youth, and in the iron age when divine guidance is withdrawn, humanity goes from youth to age. Spiritual humanity prevails in the first, earthly in the second. The terminal age of the cycle is situated at the greatest remove from the divine Principle, manifesting as widespread blind materialism which results from the closing off of the Imagination or spiritual intellect. At the darkest juncture, the reversal of the gyres occurs, indicated in "The Mental Traveller" with the lines, "They cry 'The Babe! the babe is born!'/ And flee away on Every side." For both Yeats and Blake the beginning of the Christian era was characterized by suprarational as well as irrational energies that inverted rational Rome. Likewise, for Yeats the turning of the gyres in our own era is marked by Dionysian destruction and rebirth. As he writes in his early story "The Adoration of the Magi": "Perhaps Christianity was good and the world liked it, so now it is going away and the Immortals are beginning to awake."[6] That is, Christianity as the unifying civilizational principle of the West (Christendom) has been passing for a while now, however much the Christian religion is still vital for many.

The opening poem in Yeats's play *The Resurrection* (1931) proclaims the beginning of the Christian epoch under the symbolism of the sacrifice of Dionysus-Jesus, in images like those which Blake uses near the opening of "A Mental Traveller" ("She binds iron thorns around his head, / She pierces both his hands and feet . . ."). The "staring virgin" in Yeats's lines below is Athena, who watches historical cycles change with the cold eye of divine wisdom:

> I saw a staring virgin stand
> Where holy Dionysus died,
> And tear the heart out of his side,
> And lay the heart upon her hand
> And bear that beating heart away;
> And then did all the Muses sing
> Of Magnus Annus at the spring,
> As though God's death were but a play.

In *The Resurrection*, after Jesus' crucifixion a Greek and a Hebrew argue about the divinity of Christ. The philosopher-Greek doesn't believe a divinity can be subject to mortality; he thinks it blasphemous to say a god can be born of a woman. A Syrian rushes in as the Greek and Hebrew are

6. First published in 1897; cited from Yeats, *Mythologies*, 313–14.

conversing, and announces Christ has risen. Then the figure of the risen Christ enters that very room. The Greek surmises it is merely the phantom of Jesus, not his actual body. He believes Jesus never had a human body and that, because a phantom could not have moved the tombstone, the Romans must have rolled it back. But the Syrian asks, "What if there is something it cannot explain, something more important than anything else? . . . What if there is always something that lies outside knowledge, outside order? What if at the moment when knowledge and order seem complete that something appears? . . . What if the irrational return? What if the circle begin again?"[7] The Greek says he will try to touch the figure, expecting his hand to pass right through, but when he reaches to touch Jesus he screams, "The heart of a phantom is beating!" The force of Yeats's play resides in this shock of discovering that a human heart, mortal and suffering, lies at the very center of this supernatural drama about historical change. Part II of the above poem, with which the play ends, confirms that "Whatever flames upon the night / Man's own resinous heart has fed."

In our own era, according to Yeats's system, with modernist rationalism having sown the seeds of secular doubt throughout the world, the irrational returns and the cycle begins yet again. The widespread alienation from religious faiths and traditional wisdom, even among individuals who are devout by nature, is a function of the turning of gyres and the dissolution of the unifying principle of civilization. It is one of the openings into what Yeats in his late sonnet "Meru" called the coming "desolation of reality," an idea broached also in his journal on February 12, 1909: "All civilization is held together by the suggestions of an invisible hypnotist—by artificially created illusions. The knowledge of reality is always in some measure a secret knowledge. It is a kind of death."[8] As Yeats's magus-trickster persona Michael Robartes (who is probably based on his friend MacGregor Mathers, author of the manifesto for the Order of the Golden Dawn) puts it in *A Vision,* the late autumn of a civilizational phase signals a "coming terror," as the invisible realities that bind society break apart. Yeats's remarkable early story "*Rosa Alchemica*" represents this terror, with villagers rioting and Michael Robartes getting killed in the chaos at the story's end. In the story, Robartes has come to initiate the narrator (who is clearly based on Yeats

7. Yeats, *Collected Plays*, 371. All quotations from Yeats's plays are taken from this edition.

8. Yeats, "Estrangement: Extracts from a Diary Kept in 1909," in *Autobiographies*, 356.

himself) into the Order of the Alchemical Rose. The two arrive at the west coast of Ireland, where there is a square ancient-looking house at the end of a dilapidated pier, which Robartes says is the Temple of the Alchemical Rose. There follows a striking prophetic passage, which suggests that the syncretic occult or magical doctrines represented by Robartes as well as the Temple of the Alchemical Rose are both symptoms and casualties of the centrifugal force of the present era. The narrator recalls:

> I was possessed with the fantasy that the sea, which kept covering it [the pier and the house] with showers of white foam, was claiming it as part of some indefinite and passionate life, which had begun to war upon our orderly and careful days, and was about to plunge the world into a night as obscure as that which followed the downfall of the classical world. One part of my mind mocked this fantastic terror, but the other, the part that still lay half plunged in vision, listened to the clash of unknown armies, and shuddered at the unimaginable fanaticism, that hung in those grey leaping waves.[9]

It is a chilling vision, which foreshadows not only the rioting villagers at the story's conclusion, when Robartes is killed, but also the arrival of the rough beast, the Antichrist (as well as, perhaps, the rising levels of the oceans caused by climate change). As Yeats wrote in *Pages from a Diary Written in Nineteen Hundred and Thirty*, "Dissatisfaction with the old idea of God cannot but overthrow our sense of order, for the new conception of reality has not even begun to develop, it is still a phantom not a child."[10] Likewise in *On the Boiler* (published posthumously in 1939) he wrote: "When a civilisation ends . . . the whole turns bottom upwards, Nietzsche's 'transvaluation of all values.'"[11] Clearly then, while Yeats was a voice for the resurgence of the soul against the lifeless abstraction and materialism of the modern world, this also involved noting the "terror" of the passage into the new historical cycle.

As we have seen, for Yeats the passing of the Christian era meant the rise of the antithetical phase, in which the classical or ancient-Irish heroic ideals of the active life would return. With Blake as his teacher, Yeats sought a nondualistic spiritual approach that views the body, as Blake wrote in *The Marriage of Heaven and Hell*, as that portion of the soul discerned by the

9. First published in 1896; cited from Yeats, *Mythologies*, 280.

10. Yeats, *Explorations*, 310.

11. Yeats, *Explorations*, 433.

five senses. Yeats's spiritual search, which was inseparable from his poetic vocation, therefore proceeded by a dialectic of opposites, a dynamic and circular or spiraling motion around a reconciling center or unity, which he came to call the Unity of Being. As he wrote in "If I Were Four-and-Twenty" (1919): "One day when I was twenty-three or twenty-four this sentence seemed to form in my head, without my willing it, much as sentences form when we are half-asleep: 'Hammer your thoughts into unity.'" In the same essay he explains that this required becoming "a man who brings to general converse, and business, character that informs varied interests," the way a cultivated nation relates "its main interests one to another" or men "in whom an intellectual patriotism is not distinct from religion." The essay concludes with Yeats's wish that Ireland's cultural and religious identity would come to be an important expression of a renewed Unity of Being.[12]

There are interesting parallels between Yeats's concept of the Unity of Being and his contemporary C. G. Jung's emphasis that *wholeness* rather than perfection is the fulfillment of the alchemical refinement of the soul, which has a special relevance in the present age. For Jung, the search for wholeness means first coming to terms with one's unconscious shadow side, which is associated with the less developed of the four functions of thinking, feeling, intuition, and sensation. It requires leaving nothing out of one's self-awareness, with the idea that the darker aspects of the psyche cannot be mastered or assimilated if they remain unacknowledged or repressed. For both Yeats and Jung, an alchemical conjunction of opposites is the goal, rather than the unilateral crushing of the dragon, as represented for instance in Christian images of St. George. Connected with this, Jung stressed the importance of integrating sexuality as an essential aspect of the life of the soul—a core human reality that Christian culture sidelined for centuries (with important exceptions such as the culture of courtly love and romance literature). Sex is central also to Yeats's spiritual and poetic journey, most memorably enshrined in his poems about Crazy Jane and the Bishop but very frequently broached throughout his work. In short, though Yeats was certainly an ardent seeker of wisdom, "the wisdom he had in mind," as the critic Richard Ellmann writes, "was not the saint's wisdom, and ... beatitude, if it implied total escape from the wheel of reincarnation, attracted but did not win him. For him the antinomies, even if transcended, must be present; the saint might avoid them, but not the poet. No lover of

12. Yeats, *Explorations*, 263–80; quotations on 263, 265.

holiness but of life."[13] In Yeats's 1926 play *The Cat and the Moon* a blind beggar symbolizes the soul, who chooses sight over blessedness, while a lame beggar symbolizes the body, who chooses a state of blessedness over being healed of his physical disability. The lame beggar eventually piggybacks a holy man whom the two beggars had encountered at a well. The saint has assured the beggar that he is a miracle and can dance if he wants to, whereupon the beggar indeed drops his crutches, dances, and can carry the saint. As Yeats says in his introduction to this play, "When the lame man takes the saint upon his back, the normal man has become one with his opposite." Ellmann comments that "the reconcilement of opposites was for Yeats a secular miracle, the key to his verse, his private system, and his life."[14]

That the inner work toward the *coincidentia oppositorum* for Jung involves paying attention to dreams, spontaneous waking images, and active imagination is a further parallel to Yeats in his Golden Dawn–inspired practices. Jung descends from the German romantics, for whom no authentic interior life is possible without giving dreams and visions their due. Since dreams are notoriously autonomous in relation to conscious doctrine and morality, and imagination is ambiguous, they have often been problematic from the orthodox religious perspective. The brilliant young eighteenth-century poet Novalis, who was a devout Christian, in his novel *Heinrich von Ofterdingen* has the main character Heinrich's father tell him, "The times are past when divine apparitions appeared in dreams, and we cannot and will not fathom the state of mind of those chosen men the Bible speaks of. The nature of dreams as well as of the world of men must have been different in those days. In the age we live in there is no longer any direct intercourse with heaven."[15] Needless to say, Novalis, Jung, Yeats, and Heinrich himself would disagree with Heinrich's father. Indeed, for Yeats "direct intercourse" with the archetypes is an essential experience of the creative personality in the antithetical phase.

Traditionalists warn of the dangers of seeking spiritual realization outside the tutelary guidance of orthodoxy and dogma based on divine revelation. Even an epitome of imaginative religious thinking such as the Sufi master Ibn 'Arabī said it is impossible to know God without following the authority of Revelation. And the Christian tradition emphasizes that true mystical realization grows out of dogma and theology (and that theology

---

13. Ellmann, *Yeats: Man and Masks*, 257.

14. Ellmann, *Yeats: Man and Masks*, 218, from which the Yeats quote is also drawn.

15. Novalis, *Henry von Ofterdingen*, 18.

in turn ultimately exists for the sake of mystical experience, union with God). Yet the fact remains that many in our time—and Yeats was one—find it difficult if not impossible to follow a simple faith in traditional doctrine or praxis, even if they wish they could. It is not necessarily a matter of individualistic rebellion but of estrangement and disaffection, which are widespread in a period of fundamental upheaval. Yeats is not a religious guide—he never claimed he was—but he is one of the great models for seeking and finding the ancient springs of poetry. For any true artist who happens to be religious, art is an inextricable part of religious devotion. Following Blake, Yeats stressed that religion itself ultimately arises from the spiritual intellect, or Jesus the Imagination, in the human breast, just as poetry does: "I know now that revelation is from the self, but from that age-long memoried self, that shapes the elaborate shell of the mollusc and the child in the womb, and that teaches the birds to make their nest; and that genius is a crisis that joins that buried self for certain moments to our trivial daily mind."[16] Poetry and spiritual realization for Yeats were therefore aspects of the same revelation of self, which, as we have seen, in the antithetical phase seeks a conjunction of opposites rather than renunciation of one side in favor of another.

Accordingly, Yeats's consistent wish was for the robust active life over the ascetic self-denying one. As critics and Yeats himself have often noted, his busy theater activity and public speaking were means by which he could discipline himself to wake up the solitary dreamer, to become a man of action vitally involved in the Irish movement for independence, interacting and having to compromise with others, developing a public speaking voice. Yeats, hating abstraction in general but especially in himself, wanted an earthy poetics and spiritual life. He sought "a movement downwards upon life, not upwards out of life."[17] As he noted approvingly of a portrait by Bernardo Strozzi of a Venetian in the National Gallery in Dublin, "his whole body thinks," while, in contrast, John Singer Sargent's portrait of Woodrow Wilson "lives only in the eyes."[18] In the last decade of his life, when Yeats wrote the introduction to Shri Purohit Swami's *An Indian Monk: His Life and Adventures*, he identified with Indian religion over orthodox Christianity, because the latter is preoccupied with sin while "the Indian asks for

16. Yeats, *The Trembling of the Veil*, in *Autobiographies*, 216–17.
17. Yeats, letter to Florence Farr, February 1906, *Letters*, 469.
18. Yeats, *The Trembling of the Veil*, in *Autobiographies*, 227.

an inspired intellect."[19] In Yeats's view, since Christian doctrine conceives of only one lifetime, saintliness and self-renunciation are overstressed—as though anything less or other is somehow illegitimate or incomplete— while the Indian believes that "kings, princes, beggars, soldiers, courtesans, and the fool by the wayside are equal to the eye of sanctity, for everybody's road is different, everybody awaits his moment."[20] Related to the insistence on embodiment and integration, Yeats often lamented that Christianity and the Bible stories were based in a land far away, the Holy Land in Judea, whereas "men once thought their own neighbourhood holy." For this reason, he turned to a Christ viewed in terms of Druidism and native Irish religion, "not shut off in dead history, but flowing, concrete, phenomenal," where Christ would be "a legitimate deduction from the Creed of St. Patrick [which,] as I think, is that Unity of Being Dante compared to a perfectly proportioned human body, Blake's 'Imagination,' what the Upanishads have named 'Self': nor is this unity distant and therefore intellectually understandable, but imminent, differing from man to man and age to age, taking upon itself pain and ugliness."[21]

Yeats first recorded the phrase "Unity of Being" in an automatic writing session on September 3, 1918, and then used it the next year, in the passage quoted above from "If I Were Four-and-Twenty." On October 13, 1919, Yeats and his wife George were instructed in an automatic writing session to read Dante's *Convivio*, and Yeats thereafter associated the idea of Unity of Being with Dante. He again invokes Unity of Being in "A People's Theatre," published near the end of 1919, which is where he first explicitly links the idea with the *Convivio*. Yeats sees in Dante something of the temper he wants to bring to the Irish theater, and writes that Dante's "study was Unity of Being, the subordination of all parts to the whole as in a perfectly proportioned human body—his own definition of beauty—and not, as with those I have described, the unity of things in the world."[22] Still later, in a 1921 letter to George Russell, Yeats says that unity is now a "cardinal principle" of his.[23] In fact, however, Dante in the *Convivio* doesn't compare Unity of Being to the "perfectly proportioned human body," so Yeats's memory of his source was faulty. Scholars have suggested that Yeats unconsciously

19. Yeats, *Essays and Introductions*, 431.
20. Yeats, *Essays and Introductions*, 436.
21. Yeats, "A General Introduction to My Work," in *Essays and Introductions*, 518.
22. Yeats, *Explorations*, 250.
23. Yeats, *Letters*, 667.

conflated *Convivio* III.viii and xv, and perhaps IV.xxv. I myself consider the last of these his most likely source, in part because its subject is nobility, especially nobility in action, as well as bodily beauty—both central notions and images in Yeats's work. If I am right, and because Yeats was such an intuitive, associative thinker, his concept of the Unity of Being might be seen as roughly synonymous with fully actualized nobility in Dante's conception of it. Here is the passage. Dante is describing how the noble nature appears in youth (up to age twenty-five, in Dante's system):

> The noble nature at this age displays not only obedience, sweetness, and a sense of shame, but also beauty and grace of body. . . . Here it should be understood that this work of nature is also necessary for our good life; for our soul must perform a large proportion of its activities by means of some part of the body, and it performs them well when the body is well ordered and disposed in all its parts. And when it is well ordered and disposed, then it is lovely in its entirety and in its parts; for the proper ordering of our members produces a beauty of I know not what marvelous harmony; and their good disposition, or health, casts a hue upon them that is pleasant to behold. Thus, to say that the noble nature beautifies its body and makes it elegant and harmonious, is simply to say that it inclines the body to order and perfection.[24]

Yeats eventually would find his greatest image for Unity of Being, as well as his ultimate guiding philosophy, in the Advaita (nondualistic) Vedānta. Until late 1931 Yeats had felt that his own way of thinking about reality was closest to that of Bishop Berkeley, but Ellmann notes that Berkeley "did not associate God's imagination and power with man's as closely as Yeats would have wished"—in other words he did not share Yeats's ideal of the heroic individual in the antithetical phase.[25] The year 1931 is when Yeats met the Indian swami Shri Purohit and learned about the transcendent and permanent Self of which the lower self, the human empirical ego, is a transient and contingent entity, one which cannot affect its Principle. The small *s* self is real in a certain sense, as an image in a mirror is real, though unreal compared to the object it is a reflection of, since it is real only to the extent that it participates in being as such. Isolated from this Principle it is pure nonentity. In the image of the Indian saint who strives to purify all that prevents this awareness and participation, "Yeats found

24. Dante, *Convivio* IV.xxv.11–13; my trans.
25. Ellmann, *Yeats: Man and Masks*, 279.

his own image of the artist who purges away the inessential to get down to the bedrock of passion."[26] Yeats and Purohit were closely associated for four years, when the swami returned to India. Yeats wrote introductions to the swami's autobiography, and to the latter's translation of Patañjali's *Aphorisms of Yoga* as well as to a partial autobiography by the swami's master. In 1936 the two were in Majorca to translate the Upanishads. In his preface to this translation of the Upanishads, Yeats wrote that our civilization at present is finding in its religious instinct the urge to satisfy "the whole man"—the holiness of monks as well as hard-riding country gentlemen, as he would put it later in "Under Ben Bulben." In Yeats's first major poem, *The Wanderings of Oisin* (1889), he opposes the Christian saint Patrick and the hero Oisin. The impenitent hero has no interest in an afterlife where he cannot bring his hunting dog and the great heroes suffer for eternity in hell, and he chastises what he sees as Patrick's repressed joie de vivre.

Yeats associated the nondualistic Indian understanding with that of early Christian Egypt and Ireland: "Saint Patrick must have found in Ireland, for he was not its first missionary, men whose Christianity had come from Egypt, and retained characteristics of those older faiths. . . . I would consider Ribh, were it not for his ideas about the Trinity, an orthodox man."[27] Ribh is a holy hermit of ancient Ireland, half-Druid half-Christian, who argues with St. Patrick in Yeats's late sequence "Supernatural Songs." Ribh states that he is reading his holy book in light that is shed by the spirits of the lovers Baile and Aillinn, who are reunited in the afterlife. This section of "Supernatural Songs," "Ribh at the Tomb of Baile and Aillinn," derives from one of the Japanese Noh plays Yeats learned about from Pound, in which a priest unites the spirits of two lovers after their death, bringing their purgatorial separation to an end. Clearly Ribh's light source signals a radical departure from orthodox Christian teaching, where *agape* not *eros* is the principle of love, and the font of light would be purely spiritual. Part V of "Supernatural Songs," "Ribh Considers Christian Love Insufficient," is a key statement about the Unity of Being.[28] The insufficiency of Christian love for Ribh lies precisely in the separation of *agape* from *eros*, the celestial from the earthy, the eternal from the temporal, the spiritual from the sexual. For Yeats, and in such traditions as the Kabbalah and Tantra, man and woman in sexual union mirror the combined masculine and feminine

26. Ellmann, *Yeats: Man and Masks*, 279.

27. Yeats, *Variorum Edition of the Poems*, 837–38.

28. On this, see Keeble, "Myself I Must Remake."

aspects of God. As Yeats puts it in a letter to Olivia Shakespear in 1933, "the sexual intercourse of angels is a conflagration of the whole being."[29] Clearly this is quite different from a crude libertine view of sex. While Yeats never relinquishes passion, at the same time he seeks a marriage of carnal and spiritual love. "Supernatural Songs" depicts this reconciliation of opposites.

On a collective level, Unity of Being makes unity of culture possible, whereas the present age, Yeats notes, is a "bundle of fragments." He longs for an age where "poet and artist confined themselves gladly to some inherited subject-matter known to the whole people." He adds that he learned the term Unity of Being originally from his father, who compared it to "a musical instrument so strung that if we touch a string all the strings murmur faintly."[30] For Yeats, modernism is a fall from the sort of unity that was found in a particularly vivid way in the early Italian Renaissance, when "men attained to personality in great numbers . . . and as men so fashioned held places of power, their nations had it too, prince and ploughman sharing that thought and feeling. . . . Then the scattering came, the seeding of the poppy, bursting of the pea-pod."[31] There is obviously some nostalgic idealization of the past in this portrait, though Yeats is not entirely off the mark. In any case, as is all too clear from twentieth-century history as well as the present time, the zeal to reestablish such unity, real or imagined, during an age of fragmentation can and does lead to authoritarian political ideologies—something Yeats was briefly associated with, writing favorably here and there of Mussolini.

Like many in the late 1920s and early to mid-1930s, Yeats idealized Italian fascism as an ideology of positive traditionalism, a healthy return to hierarchy, discipline, and the rule of the most educated.[32] He envisioned a restoration of the culture of Georgian Ireland, with its duality of peasant and noble bound by tradition. His interest in General O'Duffy, leader of the fascist Blueshirts, started in about 1933. Yeats wrote marching songs for O'Duffy's men that included such embarrassing verses as "What's equality?—Muck in the yard: / Historic Nations grow / From above to below"— words which he would regret a short time later. As Yeats came to realize, the followers of O'Duffy, who went off to fight for Franco in the Spanish Civil War, were at bottom just another mass-minded mob, acting under

---

29. Yeats, *Letters*, 805.

30. Yeats, *The Trembling of the Veil*, in *Autobiographies*, 164.

31. Yeats, *The Trembling of the Veil*, in *Autobiographies*, 227.

32. Cullingford, *Yeats, Ireland, and Fascism*, 202.

the pretext of tradition. As Yeats would put it in another song a little later, "What if the Church and the State / Are the mob that howls at the door!" As the terror of fascism and Nazism increased he no longer spoke in favor of any government. And in a letter of 1936 Yeats wrote: "Fascist, nationalist, clerical, anti-clerical are all responsible according to the number of their victims. I have not been silent, I have used the only vehicle I possess— verse. . . . 'The Second Coming' . . . was written some sixteen or seventeen years ago & foretold what is happening. . . . I am not callous, every nerve trembles with horror at what is happening in Europe, 'the ceremony of innocence is drowned.'"[33] He wrote to Ethel Mannin later that year that he now saw that fascism was yet another instance of an "artificial unity which ends every civilization"—a worthwhile consideration for certain traditionalists in our own time.[34] Yeats's late, nondualistic solution to the modernist quagmire was to accept that, as he puts it in "The Gyres" (1936–37), "all things run / On that unfashionable gyre again." We might read this as a non-Christian version, as it were, of Julian of Norwich's statement "all shall be well and all manner of thing shall be well": that however broken collective life and civilization may be at the present time, on the level of essential Reality, of God, nothing is shattered nor could it ever shatter. Yeats's affirmation of the soul's innate joy overcomes nihilistic despair, which is why he can say of the Chinese sages at the end of "Lapus Lazuli": "Their eyes mid many wrinkles, their eyes, / Their ancient, glittering eyes, are gay."

Though Yeats was uncommitted to any orthodox religious doctrine, he was aware of the significance and importance of traditional teachings, and he was deeply indebted to the Christian tradition—even indirectly in his conflicted rebellion against it. At the same time he valued great poetry on a par with the revelations of religion, and believed that living tradition in our age may be more available from certain artists, and by being actively engaged in the arts, than from the majority of preachers. In short, since the arts are one way still available of "conversing with Paradise," in Blake's phrase, they can have a religious function. Yeats did not believe in the religion of art in the decadent sense—indeed, he criticized his poet-friends in the Rhymers' Club for making poetry an end in itself—but felt that some great masters are "granted by divine favour a vision of the unfallen world from which others are kept apart," and by means of such artists, the

---

33. Quoted in Ellmann, *Yeats: Man and Masks*, 278.
34. Yeats, *Letters*, 869.

separation between religion and art dissolves.[35] Both Blake and Shelley were profoundly spiritual, yet they rejected the religious institutions of their day for their superficiality and moralism. From Blake and Shelley, Yeats models his theme of the modern poet taking on the lapsed function of the priest. Yeats was strongly influenced as well in his conception of the poet's priestly function by the image of the *fili* of ancient Ireland.[36] The *file* was a poet but also a scholar and guardian of traditional knowledge, a prophet and seer with divinatory powers, whose origins have been associated by some with the Druids of the pre-Christian Celts. These associations have led some to conceive of a conflict between Irish poets and the Church. The immemorial clash between Christian clerics and unruly poets is a point that Yeats delightedly picks up on in his early story "The Crucifixion of the Outcast," where the outcast poet is crucified, not by society but by the "cowardly and tyrannous race of monks, . . . haters of life and joy."[37] And in a number of Yeats's plays (for example, *The Countess Cathleen* and *The King's Threshold*), the poet-prophet represents an ideal in which second sight and lusty living are privileged over Christian charity and self-effacement.

Poets seek the living imagination, which is bound up with *eros* and the body and expresses itself in images not abstract language. As Yeats writes in *Per Amica Silentia Lunae,* "we who are poets and artists, not being permitted to shoot beyond the tangible, must go from desire to weariness and so to desire again, and live but for the moment when vision comes to our weariness like terrible lightning," unlike the sage and saint, whose asceticism and renunciation of experience are total.[38] Elsewhere he writes that while the saint goes to the center of the circle, the poet and artist must remain on the circumference, "where everything comes round again," and "the poet must not seek for what is still and fixed, for that has no life for him, and if he did, his style would become cold and monotonous"[39]—exactly what we find in much spiritually or metaphysically correct but poetically lifeless verse. For Yeats the movement of our era must be toward the embodied imagination of a Chaucer, rooted in its time and place (ironically,

35. Yeats, "William Blake and His Illustrations of the *Divine Comedy*," in *Essays and Introductions,* 117.

36. Much has been written about the role of the *file* in Irish tradition. One recent discussion is that of Carey, "Learning, Imagination and Belief," 47–75 (57–60). My thanks to John Carey for sharing his insights and this article with me.

37. In *The Secret Rose,* in Yeats, *Mythologies,* 147–56.

38. Yeats, *Mythologies,* 340.

39. Yeats, *The Cutting of an Agate,* in *Essays and Introductions,* 286–88.

considering Chaucer's Continental culture): "I could not endure . . . an international art, picking stories and symbols where it pleased. Might I not, with health and good luck to aid me, create some new *Prometheus Unbound;* Patrick or Columcille, Oisin or Finn, in Prometheus' stead; and, instead of Caucasus, Cro-Patrick or Ben Bulben? Have not all races had their first unity from a mythology that marries them to rock and hill?"[40]

Since Yeats was a poet, and a great one, these reflections and deeply held beliefs are expressed in his style, his literary technique. Yeats, who was often self-conscious of being a sedentary writer "caught / In the cold snows of a dream" (as he puts it in section V of "Meditations in Time of Civil War"), rather than a vigorous horseman or soldier or man of the world, wrote that "the self-conquest of the writer who is not a man of action is style."[41] As Ellmann notes, this self-conquest was painfully slow for Yeats. It comes as a surprise at first, given the flowing quality of Yeats's verses, that he often slogged along in his writing of poems. For him, the *furor divinus* or divine madness of poetic inspiration usually manifested in time-lapse fashion. By his own account, he would compose five or six lines on a good day, and always had half his mind on hoping that someone or something would interrupt him from the labor of writing. He contrasted his painstaking method of writing with that of Douglas Hyde, who wrote in Gaelic flowingly and without apparent effort, whereas Yeats saw himself as afflicted with the painful self-consciousness of the modern mind.

Whatever Yeats's methods, there is no modern poet who achieved more fluidity and vitality in his verse. His early poet-friends—the so-called Rhymers' Club that met weekly for poetry reading and discussion at the Old Cheshire Cheese, a pub off Fleet Street in London—all went for Dante Gabriel Rossetti and William Morris as models for verse and Pater as a model for prose. Ernest Dowson, Lionel Johnson, Arthur Symons, and the others were highly polished craftsmen of mainly melancholic lyrical poetry. As Ellmann says, poetry for them "had to do only with cadence and beauty of phrase"; and Yeats's close friend Symons said, "We are concerned with nothing but impressions."[42] Theirs was, in other words, the standard fin-de-siècle decadent aesthetic. Unlike them, Yeats rejected art for art's sake, writing that "literature must be the expression of conviction, and be the

---

40. Yeats, *The Trembling of the Veil,* in *Autobiographies,* 166.
41. Quoted in Ellmann, *Yeats: Man and Masks,* 135.
42. Both quotations from Ellmann, *Yeats: Man and Masks,* 141.

garment of noble emotion, and not an end in itself."[43] And as Yeats wrote around 1890: "I was so angry with the indifference to subject, which was the commonplace of all art criticism [at that time] . . . that I could at times see nothing else but subject."[44] The scholarly and erudite Lionel Johnson believed that philosophy and religion had said all there is to say on their subjects, noted Yeats, frustrated with the lack of curiosity in the group. As Yeats puts it in his highly engaging memoir *The Trembling of the Veil*, all conversation among them had been reduced to, "'Do you like So-and-so's last book?' 'No, I prefer the book before it.'"[45]

Yeats soon was breaking from their influence and their Pre-Raphaelite models, whose "elaborate rhythms," as Ellmann writes, "suited their strange subjects, and closed off hermetically the world of their poems from the contemporary world."[46] Yeats rejected their self-consciously poetical diction. Perhaps recalling Blake's injunction that clear and definite lines in drawing or painting convey spiritual energy, Yeats said that "all ancient vision was definite and precise," not dreamy and vague as his own poetry had been up to that point. In a letter to Fiona MacLeod in 1901 Yeats says that poetic style should seek simplicity, "self-effacing rhythm and language," and expression "like a tumbler of water rather than a cup of wine." And he adds that in his own verse he has to make "everything very hard and clear. . . . It is like riding a wild horse. If one's hands fumble or one's knees loosen one is thrown."[47] In doing so he would have to battle for many years against his early tendencies.

This stylistic awakening for Yeats is expressed in his watershed poem "Adam's Curse," published in 1902. In this poem Yeats reproduces for the first time, in Ellmann's succinct formulation, "ordinary conversation in selected, heightened form."[48] Yeats uses down-to-earth language he would have avoided in his earlier poetry:

> Better go down upon your marrow-bones
> And scrub a kitchen pavement, or break stones
> Like an old pauper, in all kinds of weather;
> For to articulate sweet sounds together

43. Quoted in Ellmann, *Yeats: Man and Masks*, 142.

44. Quoted in Yeats, *The Poems*, ed. Albright, xxv.

45. Yeats, *Autobiographies*, 147–49.

46. Ellmann, *Yeats: Man and Masks*, 136.

47. Yeats, *Letters*, 357–58.

48. Ellmann, *Identity of Yeats*, 152.

Is to work harder than all these, and yet
Be thought an idler by the noisy set
Of bankers, schoolmasters, and clergymen
The martyrs call the world.

And "Adam's Curse" includes other stylistic features that would become common in Yeats's mature work: loosened rhythms, abrupt interjections of conversational phrases, and imperfect rhymes.

As early as the period just after the publication of *The Wanderings of Oisin* in 1889, Yeats had been determined to make "ordinary modern speech" the staple of his poetry. A few months after *Oisin's* publication, Yeats was already changing phrases like "Footing in the feeble glow" to "Dancing by the window glow" and "Hangs o'er all the wooded earth" to "Overhangs the wooded earth." He purged his poetry of archaisms such as *o'er, yore,* or *ere.*[49] Many have noted that Yeats learned to make himself into a public figure by speaking to an audience. As mentioned earlier, before his public-speaking and theater activity, he had been writing mainly for other poets or for would-be poets. Edwin Muir said in a lecture on Yeats in the 1950s: "A poet who regards poetry as a métier which must not be disturbed by anything outside it is not fully human, but a sort of specialist; with the most honorable intentions he cuts himself off from the life which would fructify his art."[50] Again, we see the theme that occurs so frequently in Yeats: the search for wholeness, the integration of life and art. To keep himself honest in his composition of poetry, Yeats often wrote out a prose draft of the verses or stanza he was working on, forcing himself to shun poeticisms and find a natural voice that was still poetic. As Yeats noted in 1934, reflecting back on his poetic development, "In later years, through much knowledge of the stage, through the exfoliation of my own style, I learnt that occasional prosaic words gave the impression of an active man speaking." And he recalls how in revising his early poems he has changed such phrases as "'the curd-pale moon' to 'the brilliant moon,' so that all might seem, as it were, remembered with indifference, except some one vivid image."[51] The word *indifference* is significant in that it describes the ideal comportment of the courtier in Castiglione's Renaissance book on the topic, which Yeats greatly admired: *sprezzatura,* elegant poise, mastery that

49. Ellmann, *Identity of Yeats,* 119; the examples in the preceding sentence are also provided by Ellmann here.

50. Muir, "W. B. Yeats," in *The Estate of Poetry,* 51.

51. Yeats, *Dramatis Personae,* in *Autobiographies,* 321.

seems effortless, was the mark of the man at home in the world—and Yeats wanted above all for his poems to be at home in the world. Is this not the literary equivalent of Unity of Being?

Yeats was aiming, as he says in a letter to his father in 1913 using words that Pound could have written, for poetry to have a speech so natural "that the hearer would feel the presence of a man thinking and feeling."[52] He had moved away from what he called the "mood of pure contemplation of beauty," and from seeking "essences" to seeking "merely to lighten the mind of some burden of love or bitterness thrown upon it by the events of life," and he called this new poetry "personal utterance."[53] Yeats now avoided verbs like *sigh, wane, brood, weep,* replacing them with active verbs. Seeking more of a sense of action in the poetic line, he suggested a change of another poet's verse, "The dawn stands suddenly beside my bed," to "The Dawn runs suddenly up to my bed." He shunned empty rhetoric (insincere, high-flown language) and abstraction, where ideas are for their own sake and not "projections of human personality."[54]

In all of this work on his poetic expression, Yeats was aspiring, sometimes lucidly and sometimes in a muddled way, for the thought that "Thinks in a marrow-bone" (as he wrote in "A Prayer for Old Age"), though it would take many years of work to achieve it in a steady way. Pound's modernizing influence came with its full force during the winters of 1913–16, in a cottage in Ashdown Forest in Sussex, where Pound acted as Yeats's secretary. In 1909 Pound had considered Yeats the best poet writing in English though his style was out of date. Pound thought the poet must be "modern," by which he meant clear, precise, eliminating abstraction, getting rid of words not justifiable by sense as well as sound: hard and concrete, like a statue of Jacob Epstein, rather than like an impressionistic piano composition by Claude Debussy. Pound was hardly immune to hyperbole and self-aggrandizement, and actually Yeats was in some ways more modern, in these terms, ten years before Pound. Pound's poem "The Tree" (1907 or 1908) imitates the loose line of an early draft of Yeats's "He Thinks of His Past Greatness When a Part of the Constellations of Heaven" (1898), but Pound retains archaisms and syntactical inversions while Yeats had

52. Yeats, *Letters,* 583.

53. Yeats, *The Trembling of the Veil,* in *Autobiographies,* 128; "mood . . . beauty" is quoted from Ellmann, *Identity of Yeats,* 128. The rest of this paragraph draws on those pages in Ellmann, 116–45.

54. As Ellmann puts it in *Identity of Yeats,* 132.

not.[55] Be that as it may, in Ashdown Forest Pound critiqued Yeats's poetry, pointing out words and phrases too reminiscent of the 1890s. Yeats's great first play based on Noh theater (which he had also learned about through Pound), *At the Hawk's Well* (1917), is an early outcome of this purging of style and of abstraction. But the tone is no one's but Yeats's, as in the stoically beautiful lines,

> I call to the eye of the mind
> A well long choked up and dry
> And boughs long stripped by the wind,
> And I call to the mind's eye
> Pallor of an ivory face,
> Its lofty dissolute air,
> A man climbing up to a place
> The salt sea wind has left bare.

As we have seen, Yeats aspired to emulate in his art and life the men of action he so admired. His theater business and Irish-cultural activism, as well as his life in politics later on, forced him to become more practical, more connected to others, more direct in his speech to them, similar to how his master the visionary Blake was grounded by his business as an engraver. Yeats would observe that the body has clearer and more effectual thoughts than the brain, and all good art must make our thought "rush out to the edges of our flesh . . . whether the Victory of Samothrace which reminds the soles of our feet of swiftness, or the *Odyssey* that would send us out under the salt wind."[56] As Daniel Albright observes, Yeats's poetry became so kinesthetic that it was as if words "could be the magical equivalent of a human body."[57] It is intriguing to consider this lovely insight in light of Yeats's association of the Unity of Being with the perfectly proportioned human body.

Importantly, as the noble nature of that body suggests, Yeats's poetic language was not simply "common speech." Yeats at times says that his poetry would use the "syntax of common life," rejecting archaisms and inversions for "common syntax," but Ellmann notes that in fact Yeats placed "extraordinary syntax . . . in the mouths of . . . beggars and hermits"—for example, after a beggar stumbles on a road he says, "Were it not / I have a lucky wooden shin / I had been hurt"—and that the Yeatsian beggar

---

55. Ellmann, *Identity of Yeats*, 126–27.

56. Yeats, "The Thinking of the Body," in *Essays and Introductions*, 292.

57. Yeats, *Poems*, ed. Albright, xxix.

utters "three subjunctive clauses for every colloquialism like 'down in the mouth.' "[58] Yeats often uses a stylized word order: for example, "And should they paint or write" and "Who, were it proved he lies" and "I thought not more was needed / Youth to prolong." And he combines the distant and familiar, exalted diction and homely images, such as in this epigram,

> You say, as I have often given tongue
> In praise of what another's said or sung,
> 'Twere politic to do the like by these;
> But was there ever dog that praised his fleas?

Note how the last line uses a high oratorical wording in "But was there ever," before dropping to the homely image that ends the poem. And even his modern-sounding concreteness at times had a traditional source, as where he adapts from Erasmus the metaphor of "a post the passing dogs defile" in a poem at the end of his 1914 collection *Responsibilities*. Yeats sought a seamless integration in his poetry between tradition and the uprooted present, the stylized and the spontaneous. Having achieved this hard-won integration to a remarkable degree, Yeats would write near the end of his life:

> I tried to make the language of poetry coincide with that of passionate, normal speech. I wanted to write in whatever language comes most naturally when we soliloquise, as I do all day long, upon the events of our own lives or of any life where we can see ourselves for the moment. . . . It was a long time before I had made a language to my liking; I began to make it when I discovered some twenty years ago that I must seek, not as Wordsworth thought, words in common use, but a powerful and passionate syntax, and a complete coincidence between period and stanza. Because I need a passionate syntax for passionate subject-matter I compel myself to accept those traditional metres that have developed with the language. . . . If I wrote of personal love or sorrow in free verse, or in any rhythm that left it unchanged, amid all its accidence, I would be full of self-contempt because of my egotism and indiscretion, and foresee the boredom of my reader. . . . Talk to me of originality and I will turn on you with rage. I am a crowd, I am a lonely man, I am nothing. Ancient salt is best packing.[59]

---

58. Ellmann, *Identity of Yeats*, 133–35, is the source for this and the remainder of the paragraph until the final quotation.

59. Yeats, "A General Introduction to My Work," in *Essays and Introductions*, 521–23.

The Nazarene in Vernon Watkins's Ear

And from light's maze uncoil the magic seas,
Assembling with new time the perished fable.

THE EPIGRAPH IS FROM Vernon Watkins's long poem "Sea-Music for My Sister Travelling," in his second collection, *The Lamp and the Veil* (1945). I chose these lines because they can be read as a fanciful sketch of Watkins's work as a whole: inspired by the sea and finding in imagination and the music of poetry the eternal present, or redeemed time, of what Edwin Muir called the *fable* of a life, its archetype and vertical reality, complementing the temporal and horizontal biography of a life *story*.

Composed of lines and stanzas of varying lengths, the movement of "Sea-Music" is effusive and fluid. It appears that Watkins designed it to imitate the swing of the sea—flowing, shape-shifting, and billowing. The images metamorphose like the shapes of light on waves.

> O, the sea turns, and now your eyes look in.
> Now, a born girl above the unborn girl,
> You watch the waters spin,
> Watch the cold shuttle of the dead
> Winding the fearful thread,
> Scattered in drift of sunbeams and the spindrift whirl . . .[1]

The poem continues with run-on sentences and sharp enjambments (line breaks in the middle of grammatical units), evoking an array of marine

---

1. All quotations from Watkins's poetry are taken from the Golgonooza edition of *Collected Poems*.

phenomena, from the tropical South to the polar North. The narrative returns repeatedly to the image of dolphins following a ship; their graceful threading of the water becomes a figure for the movement of the poem itself and therefore of the imagination. It climaxes with an image of rivers flowing back to the sea, a traditional symbol for multiplicity returning to the One: "Swollen rivers run to find their principle in that first drop / That is not theirs but out of nothing fell, / Moving to time from nothing: did they find it, time would stop." The paucity of linear narrative, of cause-and-effect, creates shifting sea-like conditions for the reasoning mind of the reader, like walking wobbly on deck a heaving ship.

I usually find that I need to reread Watkins's poems to find my way into them. His meaning is rarely visible to a first glance, or even a second one, but has to be read laterally, as it were, with the eyes of one's skin. As Richard Ramsbotham has aptly put it, Watkins's "poetry only reveals itself when we respond to it musically."[2] Nearly always this effort is doubly repaid. One of Watkins's strengths throughout his work is his ability to surrender to the current of imagery, which, while impossible to grab hold of, nevertheless coheres in its layering and echoing of motifs. Kathleen Raine wrote in her seminal essay on Watkins in 1964 that the "Celtic genius" has a "characteristic evanescence, melting and mingling of contours and planes of reality"; and she quotes David Jones, who describes the Celtic imagination as a "half aquatic world . . . it introduces a feeling of transparency and interpenetration of one element with another, of transposition and metamorphosis."[3] Watkins spins out his poetic matter by contemplative immersion in poetic intuition, guided and formed by the linguistic and imaginal patterns, like currents, that it finds.

Despite his relative obscurity at present compared to his reputation during his lifetime, Watkins is surely a major poet: for the richness of his language and music, the marvel of his imagery, the virtuosity of his technique, and the depth and breadth of what he has to say.[4] Watkins may be one of the few poets after Yeats "to emulate or approach [Yeats's] poetic

---

2. Ramsbotham, introduction to Watkins, *New Selected Poems*, xvi.

3. Raine, "Vernon Watkins and the Bardic Tradition" (1964), in *Defending Ancient Springs*, 17–34; 25. Raine took the title of her book from Watkins's poem "Art and the Ravens," which had appeared in *The Death Bell: Poems and Ballads* (1954): "Nothing can live so wild / As those ambitious wings / Majestic, for love's child / Defending ancient springs."

4. On Watkins's critical neglect and misinterpretation since his death, see Ramsbotham, introduction to *New Selected Poems*, xi–xv and xxiv–xxv.

skills";[5] and although Yeats's influence on Watkins's poetry was sometimes too conspicuous, Watkins grew into his own mastery, with a style quite distinct from that of the Irish poet. The variety and beauty of his meters and rhythms are astonishing; he is a modern master of verse form, with few peers in this regard. Reading through his *Collected Poems*, we encounter a constantly varying flora and fauna of poetic techniques, with an ear attuned to the exigencies of the subject matter and the emotional content of the poem at hand. The formal variety gives his oeuvre an overall sense of being a restless search-in-progress, always receptive to poetic promptings. Unusual in our time, Watkins's openness is generally expressed via a "formalist" poetics. In contrast to most modern and postmodern poetic practice, he generally commits to the pattern of the poem once it has been established, letting this be one of his guides for where the poem wants to go. Despite the tendency of many contemporary poets to think of meter and rhyme as stifling constraints, Watkins is aware that at their best and in the right hands they are vital technologies of the imagination. He said in an interview only a few months before his death in 1967 that he generally found writing in fixed metrical form necessary to his imagination, and that one critic had commented, "each new book of Vernon Watkins is more old fashioned than the last." But, responded Watkins: "I've never cared much about fashion," and "a poet has to think in terms of centuries."[6] As he put it more aphoristically elsewhere, "A true style cannot be learnt from contemporaries."[7]

VERNON WATKINS WAS BORN in Maesteg, Glamorgan, South Wales, in 1906. When his father, a manager for Lloyds Bank, was transferred to a branch in Swansea, the Watkins family moved to the Gower Peninsula—the features of which would appear in so many of Watkins's poems. Vernon attended public school at Repton, in Derbyshire, a school about which he would write a fine dedicatory poem ("Revisited Waters"; collected in *Affinities*, 1962) for its quatercentenary in 1957. He then went to Magdalene College, Cambridge, but left after less than a year—a decision that Raine heartily endorses in her 1964 essay: "He chose tradition (vital memory) as against

5. As Kathleen Raine says in "Yeats's Singing School: A Personal Acknowledgement," in *Yeats the Initiate*, 446.

6. Interview with George Thomas, in *Vernon Watkins on Dylan Thomas*, 128.

7. Watkins, "Aphorisms," in *Vernon Watkins on Dylan Thomas*, 18.

education, and inspiration against the new positivist spirit of the age." Most people in the modern world are "exiled beyond all possibility of return to ancestral roots," but Watkins, through his parents, was still within earshot of Welsh tradition.[8] He moved back to Wales and entered the banking business of his father as a junior clerk in Cardiff, but soon after this, at about twenty-three years of age, he suffered a mental breakdown which proved to be, as his widow Gwen Watkins has said, "the defining experience of his life."[9] On his return home to Gower he was transferred to a branch of Lloyds in Swansea, and would go on to serve as a bank clerk there for nearly forty years, retiring in 1966. Watkins lived on the Pennard Cliffs outside Swansea on the South Gower peninsula throughout these years. He served in the Royal Airforce from 1941 to 1946. During his time in the RAF Intelligence, he met his future wife, Gwen, whom he married in London in October 1944 and with whom he would have five children. Dylan Thomas, Watkins's close friend whom he had first met in early 1935, was supposed to have been Watkins's best man, yet he never showed up for the celebration. A year after his retirement from Lloyds, Watkins took an offer from the University of Washington to be a visiting professor of poetry. He died of a heart attack in October 1967, shortly after arriving in Seattle, during a game of tennis—a lifelong passion of his.[10]

Watkins's breakdown in his youth amounted to a conversion experience by means of a trial by fire—Watkins himself called it a "revolution of sensibility." Years after the crisis he wrote that he had learned something "no volumes can explain . . . man is transformed"; his biographer, Richard Ramsbotham, refers to it as a near-death experience, more breakthrough than breakdown.[11] After this life-changing event, Watkins destroyed almost everything he had written up to that point—reportedly some two thousand poems. As Watkins would later put it, he "could never again write a

8. Raine, "Vernon Watkins and the Bardic Tradition," in *Defending Ancient Springs*, 18. His great early poem "Ballad of the Mari Lwyd," in the eponymous volume, draws on an ancient ritual in this tradition as performed in his father's native village.

9. Quoted on a BBC documentary about Watkins, "Swansea's Other Poet," hosted by Rowan Williams.

10. The first full biography of Watkins was published in October 2020: Ramsbotham, *An Exact Mystery*. This book came out after I had written the penultimate draft of this essay, to which I have made only a couple of small revisions since reading it.

11. This comment is from the BBC documentary cited above. The Ramsbotham biography cited in the preceding note considers the background to this decisive moment in Watkins's life in much detail.

poem which would be dominated by time,"[12] although a complete picture of Watkins's poetry would observe that it arises from an awareness that the spiritual or "transcendent" world is right here and now, in life as it is, once the doors of our perception have been cleansed.[13] The culmination of Watkins's actually quite terrifying vision was a direct experience of Christ as Savior and Redeemer. For Christians, Christ is God in His aspect of humbling Himself to take on the flesh of mortal creatures; no Manichaean dualism is possible when this is rightly grasped. Indeed, Watkins grew ever more deeply into this core truth of his faith, regularly attending the rustic Pennard Church near his home. Some forty years later, near the time of his death, he commented about his youthful breakdown: "I've been shown a great thing, I don't need to defend it." Rather than rationalizing or trying to explain it, he expressed it beautifully in a number of poems; for example, in "The Replica" (collected in *Cypress and Acacia*, 1959), in lines that declaim a specifically Christian gnosis:

> For in that dark the greatest light was born
> Which, if man sees, then time is overthrown,
> And afterwards all acts are qualified
> By knowledge of that interval of glory: . . .
> . . .
> Transmitted there by lighting majesty,
> The replica, reborn, of Christian love.

When Watkins writes on the Christian theme of redemption in the poem "Good Friday" (also in *Cypress and Acacia*), what is redeemed is fallen, desacralized time: "Day must die here that day may break." Watkins expresses the redemption of time through the Passion of Christ. The emphasis is on incarnation and full surrender to the dark moment of God's sacrifice:

> Not in the speculative skies
> Instruction lies,
> But in the nails of darkness driven
> Into these hands which hold up heaven.

12. Watkins, "Poetry and Experience," in *Vernon Watkins on Dylan Thomas*, 156.

13. Ramsbotham calls this the "paradox" of Watkins's vision (see introduction to *New Selected Poems*, xx–xxiv): "Despite his central, early experience of a reality beyond space and time, the direction of his spirituality and his poetry, as they evolved, was towards an ever-deepening relationship with the earth—with nature, with history and with other human beings" (xxi).

In "A Prayer Against Time," collected in *The Ballad of Mari Lwyd* (his first collection, 1941), the poet petitions God for his suffering to be free of time's tyranny, since the alternative would be a violation of "Tears that I owe to Thee." The poem "Good Friday" dramatizes this, emphasizing the necessity of taking up one's cross and following Christ as the means of redeeming time even as one is mortally subject to it.

The poem "Mana," also in Watkins's first book, is a meditation on death and resurrection, the eternal now within the Heraclitean flux. Contemplating a tomb, the poet writes,

> When smoke's white blooms have seeded from the bones,
> When creeds of flame have crossed the sacrificial breast,
> The twitching ashes wait
> For those light syllables less than undertones
> Murderous, immediate,
> Caressing nearer than love's hand caressed,
> At whose command Death runs, at whose behest
> Sleep claps two stones.

Besides the compact power of the opening metaphor—cremation as a kind of blossoming and seeding—the delicate modulation of this passage shows that Watkins had already achieved considerable mastery of his craft. The poem opens with the stately rhythms of a pentameter and then a hexameter verse, followed by rapidly enjambed shorter lines. Also, the eight-line stanza uses three rhymes, in an ABCACBBA pattern, which the six-stanza poem repeats, each stanza using the B rhymes of the previous stanza in the A position—so stanza 2 of this poem opens, "Here sacred walls surround their withered guest." The result is an intricate pattern that imitates the very "seeding" referred to in the opening line. While the bitterness of death and the grief of being bound on time's wheel permeate the poem, Watkins concludes it with a premonition of something "far more deeply interfused" (to use Wordsworth's phrase), an eternal seed planted in every moment of time:

> Tree of all leaves, skin of all creatures, ground
> Where eyes still seek an image in the Godhead made,
> Our hands have tied
> What death must now undo without a sound;
> But you, the bride
> Of morning, shining through the yew-tree's shade,
> Hold with unique unrest, so naked laid,
> Our eyes spellbound.

The phrase "unique unrest," with its visually similar yet aurally contrasting words is a deceptively simple poetic synthesis, like an epithet for spiritual vigilance.

A difference between Watkins's poems in his earlier volumes, such as this, and those in his later collections is the greater frequency in the latter of the same theme being treated in explicitly Christian terms. In the fine sonnet "The Yew-Tree," collected in *The Lady with the Unicorn* (1948), the speaker is in a graveyard, reflecting on both the dead and those in the past who mourned their dead. He wonders whether the dead should simply remain that way—what need is there for resurrection?—but then he hears the mourners, those for whom the dead were beloved. One of these says, "O, who will lift this lost, loved head, / Crowned with flowers fading, whose quick colours pray?" The answer comes from the Gospel story of the good thief, on the cross next to Jesus: resurrection is a manifestation of divine mercy, which "kills grief":

> I hear that good thief say:
> "Lord, for no wrong Thou diest, but justly we."
> That word kills grief, and through the dark-boughed tree
> Gives to each dead his resurrection day.

Watkins's 1954 collection *The Death Bell* is predominantly a meditation on death and resurrection, a recognition of the pain of death and loss, as well as an evocation of spiritual realities not subject to time and death. The great title poem opens with an explicit acknowledgment of mortality, in the form of God made flesh, the birth of Christ, which is "Love that fulfils the law / Figured in limbs, not wings," and a statement of faith in Christ that nevertheless recognizes the knoll of the death bell: "For this bell tolls to birth"—that is, the gong of the bell signals the promise of resurrection as well as the knowledge of mortality and death. As Dante says in canto XXV of *Paradiso*, where St. James examines Dante on the theological virtue of hope, Christian hope resides in the promise of resurrection. And Watkins in his poem makes an explicit connection between resurrection and poetry, which, in this world, is a form of life after death:

> Since death and birth obey
> One measured harmony,
> Shall not the lyre outweigh
> The grief-enfolding sea?

As Watkins writes in his note at the end of *Death Bell*'s title poem: "The resurrection of the body is assured, not by the instinct of self-preservation, but by the moment of loss, of the whole man's recurrent willingness to lose himself to an act of love." Also in *Death Bell*, the long poem "Niobe" shows that the grief and surrender to death's inexorableness that run throughout this collection have their origin in the events of World War II, the katabasis of which, suggests the poem, is potentially a forceful catalyst for rebirth: "If we shall live, it must be from this rock / The stream shall break."[14] Elsewhere in *Death Bell*, in the poem "Pledges to Darkness," the poet explicitly states his allegiance to the mortal and ephemeral, even as he seeks for the transcendent that is immanent within it.

Though Christian themes arise frequently in Watkins's work, Rowan Williams has asked whether Watkins was a conventional believer, or someone who knew the language and symbols of religion without quite wanting to pin down what his views were about them.[15] In my view, the answer to this is that Watkins was an orthodox practicing Christian with a natural bent for metaphysical reflection and hermetic thought. Though he was not an adherent per se of the modern Perennialist school, there is something of the "transcendental unity" of religious experience in his approach to both poetry and Christianity. In this, Watkins is closer to Blake or a Christian-romantic such as Novalis than to recent Anglophone Christian poets such as his fellow Welshman R. S. Thomas. Plato and Plotinus, Dante and Shelley and Hölderlin—these were enduring sources for Watkins's poetic and intellectual sustenance. His view of the creation is both incarnational and theophanic, the epitome of which is the incarnation of God in Christ. Many of Watkins's poems contemplate natural phenomena as hermetic signs or openings to metaphysical realities: "I marvel at the beauty of landscape, but I never think of it as a theme for poetry until I read metaphysical symbols behind what I see."[16] Some recent critics have viewed this as an escapist tendency on Watkins's part to hurry from empirical to internal experience[17]— but this is to impose standard contemporary ignorance about metaphysical

---

14. As Richard Ramsbotham observes in his introduction to *New Selected Poems*, xviii–xix, Watkins's "ability to address the situation of his time," for example with profound insight into the moral crisis of World War II, has "received almost no attention." There is indeed an undercurrent of profound grief and darkness in the poems Watkins wrote during the war.

15. From the BBC documentary "Swansea's Other Poet."

16. Quoted in Sanesi, "Vernon Watkins," 108.

17. See Ramsbotham, introduction to *New Selected Poems*, xx, for examples.

insight onto a sensibility that does not fit contemporary preconceptions. In fact, Watkins's poems can be at their most evocatively sensual (in their *musicality*, always, and often in their imagery as well) precisely when they are at their most metaphysical. What Kathleen Raine wrote about Shelley applies to Watkins as well: symbols in his poems "are gathered up with the speed of thought from the natural world which was for him the mirror in which he saw reflected the spiritual forms of an intelligible order."[18] In "Music of Colours: The Blossom Scattered," which is in *Death Bell*, Watkins explicitly states that the light evoked so often in his poems is that for which visible light is an outward sign:

> Light the saints teach us, light we learn to adore;
> Not space revealed it, but the needle's eye
> Love's dark thread holding, when we began to die.
> It was the leper's, not the bird's cry,
> Gave back that glory, made that glory more.

The leper as an occasion for the Christic miracle, and therefore for the immanence of the divine within the creaturely, is associated with this light that is not of space but is of the celestial needle's eye or *punctum*. It is the Logos, the light of love that outlasts what dies and therefore can cleanse the leper.

As a contemplative-metaphysical poet, Watkins works within the tradition of symbolic analogy. He is equally at home writing about Christ or about the Welsh bard Taliesin. He can write of Apollo and Daphne, or Nefertiti within an integral and encompassing view, the universal language of symbols. Watkins's insight into mythic imagery in various traditions makes it possible for him to utilize, for example, the stories of Naomi and Ruth from the Old Testament and the story of the Danaë from Greek myth within a single stanza and without any "syncretism" that might misleadingly conflate one tradition with another. As Raine emphasized, the language of symbols is "one language that runs right through the whole of European and, to a certain extent, world literature. One knows immediately when a poet uses the symbol of water, or whatever it may be, whether it is being used with these resonances of meaning or without"—and she names

---

18. Raine, introduction to Shelley, *Shelley*, 16. Criticism of Watkins is sometimes reminiscent of Matthew Arnold's obtuse characterization of Shelley as an "ineffectual angel."

Watkins as one who has this facility "to a certain extent," though in my view he has it to a remarkable degree.[19]

Even when his poems are on explicitly Christian themes, Watkins's symbolic language and metaphysical insight open the poem's content beyond the doctrinal parameters of Christianity per se. For example, his poem "I, Centurion" is about the centurion whose servant was healed by Jesus and who witnessed Jesus raising a young man from the dead. In this poem, Watkins has the centurion say that "All that is true in earth or sky / Begins and ends in music." And the centurion describes hearing Jesus' words:

I,

Truth and obedience being my trade,
Hearing the voice even Death obeyed,
Was smitten then by hidden strings,
Seeing this last of underlings [the servant]
Healed and made whole.

Here, the Logos is seen as the principle of healing and harmony, which is literally musical; the voice of the Logos is the music of the spheres, and is also the harmony of poetry itself, which heals with its sonorousness the way Jesus heals lepers and paralytics in the Gospels. This sense of the poem is reinforced by Watkins's placement of it in *Cypress and Acacia*, just before "In the Protestant Cemetery, Rome," which contrasts the reality of immortal verse (Keats and Shelley are buried in this cemetery) with death and temporality.

"The Song of the Good Samaritan," a poem in terza rima in *The Lady with the Unicorn*, alludes to the parable from the Gospel of Luke about a Jewish man who was assaulted by robbers on the way from Jerusalem to Jericho, stripped, beaten, and left for dead alongside the road. A priest and a Levite passed him by without helping, but a Samaritan, who normally would have been despised by Jews and considered a religious and social inferior, stopped to help him. Before Jesus tells this story, a lawyer has asked him how one attains eternal life, to which Jesus answers: "Thou shalt love the Lord thy God with thy whole heart, and with thy whole soul, and with all thy strength, and with all thy mind: and thy neighbor as thyself." But the lawyer presses Jesus further, asking, "And who is my neighbor?" The parable of the good Samaritan is Jesus' answer to this question.[20] Importantly, for understanding the sense in which Watkins is a Christian poet, he does not

19. Keeble, "An Interview," 31.

20. Luke 10:25–37.

simply allude to this story as it is to be found in the Gospel, adding a poetic insight or comment or two. Rather, he makes the familiar story strange again by retelling it in a rush of impassioned imagery and mythic associations, metaphysical insight, and the symbolic language of nature. The poem's theme is Christian mercy and compassion, through which "the era of love is born," contrasted with the survival-of-the-fittest ethos of the pre-Christian ancient world, which Watkins represents through the imagery of brute force in ancient myth, especially that of the Centaurs. In contrast, the Samaritan in Watkins's poem, embodying the Christian (and indeed universally spiritual) point of view, says that "The wound I suffer, the joy I am bearing, is he [the man robbed and left for dead]." And the ability to freely choose as opposed to compulsively act is another difference between the Samaritan and the Centaurs. As the Samaritan says in the poem:

> For they were movement itself, but mine was a choice
> Between those visions acclaimed by pride overthrown,
> And the downcast, intimate eyes . . .

Another explicitly Christian poem, "Quem Quaeritis?" ("Whom do you seek?"), collected in *Affinities*, recounts various of Christ's miracles in the voices of those whom he healed. Significantly—Watkins's collections were always artfully orchestrated—"Quem Quaeritis?" follows Watkins's great "Music of Colours: Dragonfoil and the Furnace of Colours." I will discuss the latter text first, and then suggest its connection to "Quem Quaeritis?"

The last of Watkins's three poems on the theme of the "Music of Colours," "Dragonfoil" draws on the lush imagery of a summer garden. Consisting of 101 lines, it is divided into three sections or movements: section 1 evokes the infinite variety of nature, and concludes with the symbolic source of that variety; section 2 is an inward-looking step back, elaborating on the Orpheus symbolism broached at the end of the previous section; section 3 pulls the strands of the poem together, with the realization that "All that is made here hides another making."

"Dragonfoil" is an ecstatic evocation of colorful fecund vegetation, the myriad array of color as a manifestation of divine abundance. As the poem asks, after having evoked the "Bright petal, dragonfoil, springing from the hot grass," the profusion of summer fertility and growth:

> Where were these born then, nurtured of the white light?
> Dragonfly, kingfisher breaking from the white bones,

Snows never seen, nor blackthorn boughs in winter,
Lit by what brand of a perpetual summer,
These and the field flowers?

Passages such as this are Keatsian in their inebriating imaginative sensuality, full of finely observed detail and botanical nomenclature that grounds the ecstatic contemplation of nature: tiger-lily, snake-fang, poppy, mustardseed, cornflower, bluebell, lily, iris—all the rich names beloved of the naturalist. But Watkins's naming is Adamic; it goes deeper and farther, referring the palette of colors and the textures of names to their metaphysical roots in the ever-fecund Mother, the *punctum* of generation symbolized in this poem by the white spray that rainbows out from the crashing waves on the Gower coast, as well as the myth of Orpheus and Eurydice, where absence is the source of song and nature's abundance is seen through for its secret identity with death and the underworld, the soul's pull of bereavement and longing.

Note the falling rhythms in the lines below, reminiscent of the nostalgically tinged meter of Sappho, including an adonic verse (five syllables that are stressed-unstressed-unstressed-stressed-unstressed) at the end of each stanza.

Speak: what Ophelia lies among your shadows?
Is it her music, or is it Eurydice
Gone from your bank, for there a spirit's absence
Wakens the music that was heard by Orpheus,
Lost, where the stream glides.

Far off, continually, I can hear the breakers
Falling, destroying, secret, while the rainbow,
Flying in spray, perpetuates the white light,
Ocean, kindler of us, mover and mother,
Constantly moving.

The outward show of nature is marvelous and, in fact, miraculous, not only in its ephemeral appearance but in its theophanic revelatory power. The phenomena of nature are signs conveying meanings beyond what the senses perceive. Its beauty is the expression of its beatific essence:

There the stream flies on to its own beginning,
Slips through the fresh banks, woods of their escaping,
Leaving in glory patterns of a lost world,
Leaves that are shadows of a different order,

Light, born of white light, broken by the wave's plunge
Here into colours.

The ecstatic beauty of nature in summer, when the mind is drunk on heat
and the body is awash in the flux of sensation, can engulf us like Odysseus
in the land of the lotos eaters, as the poem concludes:

Yet, not that bloom, nor any kind of foliage,
Cup, sheath or daystar, bright above the water,
Clustered forgetmenots tufted on the stream's bank,
Not one recalls the virginals of April
Heard, when the wood grieved.

. . .

Falling on gold sand, bringing all to nothing.
Fire of the struck brand hides beneath the white spray.
All life begins there, scattered by the rainbow;
Yes, and the field flowers, these deceptive blossoms,
Break from the furnace.

This brings us back to Watkins's placement of "Quem Quaeritis?" in the
collection *Cypress and Acacia*. I believe that this poem follows "Music of Co-
lours: Dragonfoil" to reinforce the notion of the divine as the ultimate source
of nature's bounty. As "Quem Quaeritis?" concludes: "They look for glory in
day, and we in gloom. / We look for Him who has overcome the tomb." This
is the answer to "Whom do you seek?" To seek anything less than the divine
source is to commit the error of pantheism, dazzled by appearances.

Watkins's gift for magical evocation is fully realized in his "Music
of Colours" poems. The title of the series exemplifies one technique that
Watkins likes to use for evoking inscapes of the outer world: synesthesia,
or expressing one sense in terms of another. In "Music of Colours: White
Blossom," which opens *The Lady with the Unicorn*, the reference to the
"Nazarene / Walking in the ear" recalls Rilke's comparison of Orpheus's
song to a tree growing in the ear of the listener:

White blossom, white, white shell; the Nazarene
Walking in the ear; white touched by souls
Who know the music by which white is seen,
Blinding white, from strings and aureoles,
Until that is not white, seen at the two poles,
Nor white the Scythian hills, nor Marlowe's queen.

Is "the music by which white is seen" related to the "sea-music" discussed at the beginning of this essay? I would say yes, since the "ear" in this passage is the "shell" in which that music may be heard. The white noise of the surf is "blinding" because it is heard not seen. Watkins has done something extraordinary in this passage, by means of his uncanny symbolic sense: the white noise of the surf is associated with the blossom, the Scythian hills, and Marlowe's queen's white skin, as expressive of their essence. And Jesus "walks in the ear" because this white is salvific white, the white of resurrection, of the purified spiritual essences of things. Only souls who know this music "by which white is seen" as the revelation that it is—that is, souls who know the Logos, the Christ—can touch this white. We know Watkins is referring to white as an image of resurrection, since he states it explicitly several lines down: "from the deluge of illusions [the flood from which Noah was saved] an unknown color is saved. // White must die black, to be born white again." Until then, what we call white is so only in a relative sense:

> The spray looked white until this snowfall.
> Now the foam is grey, the wave is dull.
> Call nothing white again, we were deceived . . .
> . . .
> If there is white, or has been white, it must have been
> When His eyes looked down and made the leper clean.

The white that is the subject of these poems, then, is primordial being, the Christic *salus* of being as such, or "Original white," as Watkins puts it near the end of the poem. Through archetypal imagery, paradox, synesthesia, and a rich tapestry of sonics, Watkins evokes the ineffable world of the nonmanifest. In *Vernon Watkins and the Spring of Vision* Dora Polk writes, in reference to this poem, that the "colours of the rainbow and imperfect white represent transient natural phenomena. Obversely, pure white, original whiteness, the perpetual transcendent life stuff, is seldom experienced by men except in epiphanic moments as at the advent of Christ, and Jove's visitation of Leda, and other moments of miraculous conception and generation"—when "all colours hurled in one," so that there is a transfiguring radiance.[21] In short, Watkins's particular Christian-metaphysical perspective is closely connected with his view of the transfiguration of the natural world in poetic vision.

21. Polk, *Vernon Watkins*, 31.

His Taliesin poems are the most direct and comprehensive expression of this Christian-hermetic approach to nature. As Richard Ramsbotham writes: "One of the great differences between Taliesin and the earlier Irish Bards is that Taliesin links his bardic union with nature with Celtic Christianity. . . . Taliesin's Celtic Christian relationship to nature is essential to Vernon Watkins's series of poems identifying himself with Taliesin." [22] In addition, Taliesin represents the "other" mind of inspiration; shaman-like, he dies and reincarnates so his knowledge is coeval with the world's creation. Brian Keeble succinctly characterizes Taliesin's import to Watkins's imagination:

> Taliesin serves the poet's purpose ideally by exemplifying the conquest of time through the reconciliation of opposites. . . . Taliesin's visionary standpoint, in which he transcends the darkening incursions of the temporal order, rests on his pagan appeal to the elemental powers of the primeval unity. In this respect Taliesin is the pivotal point around which the four basic elements of Watkins's imagination revolve: nature, pagan myth, metaphysical vision, and the Christian redemption of history. The figure of Taliesin links them all. [23]

Taliesin is the "time-conqueror" in Watkins, the "voice of the poet as oracular namer of that mutability he transcends"; he is the poetic persona who "aided the poet in shaping his conviction that the whole is present in every part." [24]

Watkins published four Taliesin poems: "Taliesin in Gower," collected in *The Death Bell*; "Taliesin and the Spring of Vision," in *Cypress and Acacia*; and "Taliesin's Voyage" and "Taliesin and the Mockers," both in *Affinities*. "Taliesin in Gower" consists of long sprawling lines, with a Blakean expansiveness: "Late I return, O violent, colossal, reverberant, eavesdropping sea. / My country is here. I am foal and violet. Hawthorn breaks from my hands." The bard is the voice of the elements, the namer of things. Taliesin is Orphic in the power of his song to call things forth. He is a Welsh Adam who is also protean ("I have passed through a million changes"). In these poems, Watkins's profound identity with the Gower landscape has its fullest expression: "I am nearer the rising pewit's call than the shiver of her own wing. / I ascend in the loud waves' thunder." The things of the natural

22. Ramsbotham, *Exact Mystery*, 260 n. 13.

23. Keeble, *Vernon Watkins*, 15–16.

24. Keeble, *Vernon Watkins*, 16, 17.

world are words in the book of creation, the inner meanings of which the poetic imagination may rejuvenate: "In the hunter's quarry this landscape died; my vision restores it again. / These stones are prayers; every boulder is hung on a breath's miraculous birth." The poem concludes with the image of Watkins-Taliesin-Orpheus resolving to dedicate himself to his craft, figured here as the making of his lyre:

> I celebrate you, marvellous forms. But first I must cut the wood,
> Exactly measure the strings, to make manifest what shall be.
> All Earth being weighted by an ear of corn, all heaven by a drop of blood.
> How shall I loosen this music to the listening, eavesdropping sea?

The macrocosm, Earth and Heaven, is evoked by the microcosm, corn and a drop of blood.

"Taliesin's Voyage" and "Taliesin and the Mockers" are entirely different stylistically: both written in short (dimeter) lines, the former one rhyming the second not. The first of these poems draws on the tale of Taliesin, included by Lady Charlotte Guest in *The Mabinogion*. In this story, the son of the witch Caridwen and the giant Tegid Voel, Morvran, is so ugly that Caridwen brews a potion to give him knowledge of the mysteries, prophetic insight, and poetic inspiration—all to help him gain an honorable place among the nobility. The potion must boil for a year and a day, and a young boy named Gwion Bach is given the task of stirring it for Caridwen in the magic cauldron. When three drops of the potion fall on Gwion's hand, the burning makes him put his hand to his mouth, whereby he is endowed with the wisdom and inspiration that Caridwen had intended for Morvran. Gwion flees to escape Caridwen's wrath, and they both shape-shift into various animals during the pursuit. For example, he becomes a rabbit and she a dog chasing him; when he becomes a fish and jumps into a river she becomes an otter in his pursuit. Finally, when he becomes a grain of corn she takes the shape of a hen and eats him. However, because he has already ingested the potion, he is immortal. He does not die in her; rather, she becomes pregnant, and when Gwion is born from her, Caridwen sews him in a leather bag and throws him into the ocean. The boy is rescued on a Welsh shore, and grows to become Taliesin, the bard and prophet of Wales.

In "Taliesin's Voyage," the boy is floating in his coracle on the sea—an image of inspiration, which is always timeless, within the realm of flux and change. The boy gazes up at the ravens and kestrels, and sees the axis of their gyres as well as the bonds connecting them to it:

> I, Taliesin,
> Know the cords
> Between that pin
> And the turning birds.

In all of Watkins's Taliesin poems, Taliesin is a figure for inspiration, the Imagination in the sense in which Blake used that word, the spiritual intellect which is out of time and so is present at the creation of all things, which in reality occurs at every instant. He is a vessel and mouthpiece for the Logos:

> Before men walked
> I was in these places.
> I was here
> When the mountains were laid.
>
> . . .
>
> Still upon Earth
> Was no live creature.
> Barren still
> Was the womb of the sea.
>
> Mute the features
> Slept in the rock,
> Limbs and the soul
> Inert, unbeckoned.

The voice of this poem is reminiscent of the passage in the Book of Wisdom where Wisdom says she was present at the creation ("When God prepared the heavens, I was there . . ." etc.). Dante too, in the *Convivio*, associates this Solomonic Wisdom with the Logos through whom all things were made.[25] Then comes the creation of beasts, plants, and finally, man. Next, historical events are alluded to: the building of Babel's tower, Solomon's temple (in which Taliesin says he was a lamp), the coming of Christ. The poem concludes with lines that are obviously self-referential on Watkins's part (he did not belong to any "school" of poetry and was painfully aware of being outside the positivist cultural climate):

> Mock me they will,
> Those hired musicians,
> They at Court
> Who command the schools.

25. Proverbs 8:27–30; *Convivio* III.xv.

Mock though they do,
My music stands
Before and after
Accusing silence.

"Taliesin and the Spring of Vision" is one of Watkins's greatest compositions. It gives the impression of having come to him almost whole, though by Watkins's own account he rarely composed poems this way—he generally worked through many drafts over months or years. Unusually for Watkins, the poem is written in longish lines of free verse or loose accentual verse (a regular number of beats per line but no regular pattern of stressed and unstressed syllables). The long lines and expansive cadences create a heightened prophetic tone. Also unusual for Watkins, the poem has four speaking characters or personas: Taliesin himself treading on sand on the shore; the sand, which responds to him; the third-person narrator; and invisible instructors or spirit guides.

Taliesin opens the poem by saying he is walking along the shore treading the sand that is used for hourglasses. The sand sings to him, saying Taliesin is

"my nearmost, you who have travelled the farthest,
And you are my constant, who have endured all vicissitudes
In the cradle of sea, Fate's hands, and the spinning waters.
The measure of past grief is the measure of present joy . . .
. . .
Here time's glass breaks, and the world is transfigured in music."

Note that Taliesin himself is quoting the personified sand within the frame of the poem. The sand alludes to Taliesin's having passed through a baptism of fire, grief, the trials of mortality and temporal existence. But here "time's glass breaks"—the sand is freed from its hourglass to become the shoreline and to sing, which is one manifestation of the world transfigured in music. In the next stanza, Taliesin takes "refuge under the unfledged rock," a dark cave or womb of earth, where "the rock he touched was the socket of all men's eyes, / And he touched the spring of vision." Then come these remarkable lines, which reveal Taliesin as an initiate who is free of ego's illusory separateness:

He had the mind of a fish
That moment. He knew the glitter of scale and fin.
He touched the pin of pivotal space, and he saw
One sandgrain balance the ages' cumulus cloud.

The "pin" is the *punctum*, the point upon which, as Beatrice tells Dante in the Primum Mobile in canto XXVIII of *Paradiso*, all of creation hangs. As the stanza after the next one clarifies, this place of inner vision is also the place of the soul's rebirth and of poetic inspiration:

> . . . three drops fell on his fingers,
> And Future and Past converged in a lightning flash:
> "It was we who instructed Shakespeare, who fell upon Dante's eyes,
> Who opened to Blake the Minute Particulars. We are the soul's rebirth."

But Taliesin does not forget about earthly and temporal life in his enlightenment. As the next lines open in a new stanza, "Earth's shadow hung. Taliesin said: 'The penumbra of history is terrible.'" In this life, even total mindfulness of the eternal present, of God closer than a throb of our artery, does not negate the experience of time and transience:

> Life changes, breaks, scatters. There is no sheet-anchor.
> Time reigns; yet the kingdom of love is every moment,
> Whose citizens do not age in each other's eyes.

As the latter part of this passage adds, the Spirit remains free of the ravages of time. And then come some of the most prophetic lines of Watkins's work, which affirm the abiding validity of the springs of vision, of living tradition, to restore things to their proper relations, to their balance. As Taliesin says (he himself is speaking throughout this stanza):

> In a time of darkness the pattern of life is restored
> By men who make all transience seem an illusion
> Through inward acts, acts corresponding to music.
> Their works of love leave words that do not end in the heart.

Taliesin's encounter with the springs of vision and the invisible Instructors concludes with his acceptance of his mortality, of Christian humility in emulation of Christ's own taking on of flesh and time. The prophetic, bardic spirit itself seeks baptism here; the cosmic spirit is reluctant to leave the freedom of timeless nature for human history, yet he makes the choice:

> Taliesin answered: "I have encountered the irreducible diamond
> In the rock. Yet now it is over. Omniscience is not for man.
> Christen me, therefore, that my acts in the dark may be just,
> And adapt my partial vision to the limitation of time."

The above stanza marks a major change in Watkins's poetry. There will be more poems concerned with mortality after this, and there will be more conventionally narrative, naturalistic material. The poem "A Man with a Field," for example, immediately after "Taliesin and the Spring of Vision" in *Cypress and Acacia*, clearly follows up on the latter's statement of commitment, since it is a poem written in relatively plain, direct style, in long prosy lines—though Watkins does impose a rhyme scheme on it. It is a poem about a man who has died, recalling his life: "If I close my eyes I can see a man with a load of hay / Cross this garden." Two poems after this in the same collection, "The Scythe" recalls the relics of a farm man's life. The scythe and its edge are like metonyms for the departed friend or neighbor: "Custom shall not restore / The scythe to its old place." But in memory he recalls the deceased man "Leaning above his blade / Near the long-shadowed sheaves."

The tone and focus have shifted from bardic and epiphanic vision to humble and simple recollection. As Kathleen Raine summarizes, starting with *Death Bell*, the volume before *Cypress and Acacia*, Watkins moves "from pagan rite to Christian sacrament; his lyricism tends more and more to diverge from the abundant rhapsodic image-laden poetry of his own youth and that of Dylan Thomas; his themes, as they become more austere in feeling and image at the same time become more complex and more reflective."[26] This development is described in a highly compressed and elliptical way in the poem "Three Harps," in *Cypress and Acacia*, which says that death and mortality have taught the poet how to "play this harp of bone." The godlike power of the inspired artist, represented in this poem by Daedalus and Icarus, is contrasted with the death-in-life human condition that the end of the poem evokes:

> Little for the sun I cared,
> Little for renown,
> I saw the unknown, unshared,
> True grave. So I lay down;
>
> Lay down, and closed my eyes
> To the end of all time,
> The end of birth's enterprise
> And death's small crime.
>
> Then at once the shrouded harp
> Was manifest. I began

26. Raine, "Vernon Watkins and the Bardic Tradition," in *Defending Ancient Springs*, 30.

> To touch, though pain is sharp,
> The ribs of the man.

There are three harps or modes of art in the poem: one based on emulation, one expressing loss and the mortal condition, and the one just above, "the shrouded harp," which is the visionary one that is born after spiritual death and surrender to fate, where the "ribs of the man" are touched upon or strummed into music. The idea expressed here is similar to the resolution at the end of "Taliesin and the Spring of Vision," discussed above. As Watkins will put it in "Two Sources of Life," in *Fidelities* (1968), the collection published just after his death,

> We were transfigured by the deaths of others.
> That was the spring, when first we knew our brothers
> And died into the truth which made us live.

Everything That Lives

Kathleen Raine's Prophetic Vocation

"It is I," I knew. "I am that flower, that light is I."

—KATHLEEN RAINE

I 'M USING THE WORD *prophetic* in the title of this essay in the Blakean
sense of it. Blake cites the Book of Numbers, "Would to God that all
the Lord's people were Prophets," to suggest that prophetic intuition
is not limited to a chosen few.[1] Like Blake, the poet-scholar Kathleen Raine
believed that the prophetic spirit is a capacity latent in all but asleep in
most; and the prophetic individual is one who, speaking "*from* the spirit
innate in all, *to* the spirit innate in all," calls upon the rest of us to wake up.[2]
What we wake up to is a renewed awareness of essential (spiritual) realities,
which human beings have a tendency to forget. Raine noted that we live in
a time when the prophetic voice is seldom heard or even attempted. This
is not surprising, since to speak of prophecy is nonsense from the mod-
ernist point of view, for which there is no essential spiritual reality to be

---

1. Numbers 11:29; preface to *Milton*, in *Blake: Complete Writings*, edited by Geoffrey
Keynes, 481. Subsequent citations from Blake will be to this edition, given as "K." with
the page number. Blake himself is citing Milton, from *Areopagitica*: "For now the time
seems come wherein Moses, the great prophet, may sit in heaven rejoicing to see that
memorable and glorious wish of his fulfilled, when not only our seventy elders, but all
the Lords people, are become prophets" (Milton, *Portable Milton*, 195).

2. Raine, "Poetry as Prophecy," in *Yeats and Learning of the Imagination*, 92–111
(101).

prophetic about.[3] And for Raine this omission has devastating and far-reaching consequences.

A recurrent theme in Raine's critical writings is that the rationalist-materialist mindset that dominates the modern world *inevitably* leads to a demise in poetry and the arts, since (as all the religions teach) to deny the primacy of spirit is to deny the human being as such. As Raine notes in her essay "What Is Man?" (1977), since art is produced by human beings for human use, any approach to the arts clearly must be based, implicitly or explicitly, on a theory of what human beings essentially are.[4] And if the latter is framed in materialist terms, the arts—which traditionally include all human making and industry—will be limited to maintenance, fortification, and expression of the empirical self, Blake's "worm of sixty winters," "Born in a Night to perish in a Night."[5] Society and civilization will be machines for producing wealth and stockpiles of goods, and people will be reduced to cogs that keep the machine going. Education will be an elaborate system of indoctrination into the quantitative-secular mentality, and of job training for wage slaves to perform utilitarian and artless functions.

In a world conditioned by secular reductionism, Raine says, poetry as the language of the Imagination (again in Blake's sense of the word) is bound to be undervalued, even denigrated, in favor of poetry concerned with "the observable, the immediate, and the process of change as values in themselves."[6] This mentality infiltrates not only the writing of poetry but the reading of it as well, especially in contemporary academia. Critical rationalism—often in the form of political reductionism—undermines

---

3. In this essay, when I use the words *modernist* or *modernism* I am referring to the fantasy of limitless and metaphysically rootless material progress, ultimately springing from materialist premises: the belief that matter is the ontologically fundamental reality while mind, soul, and spirit are merely epiphenomena of matter. *Modern* on the other hand simply means whatever is of the present period of time.

4. Raine, "What Is Man?" in *Inner Journey of the Poet*, 1–13. This and some others of Raine's essays cited here have been reprinted in *That Wondrous Pattern*, edited by Brian Keeble.

5. From *Europe: A Prophecy*, K. 240; and *Auguries of Innocence*, K. 434.

6. The quotation is from Raine's essay "Yeats and the Learning of Imagination," in *Yeats and Learning of the Imagination*, 21–36 (21). In a 2019 article about Raine's poetry, Carol Rumens describes how Raine's orientation marginalized her work in the contemporary cultural climate: "I neglected Raine's work for years, being more interested in poetry as the engineering of words and worldliness, of personal idiom and specific observation." As the headline of the article puts it, Raine's "mystical bent was out of tune with her times." Rumens, "Poem of the Week."

the imaginative receptivity that is essential for allowing poetry to permeate the reader's inner world. Raine's essay "Premises and Poetry" (1975) notes that modern education with its rationalist prejudices produces readers who cannot grasp the great poetry of the past. Such readers come from a different world than the one the poet inhabited, who, since certain traditional understandings of humanity were implicit in all cultures before our own, wrote about or assumed such things as the soul, beauty, and the sacred—all meaningless constructs in a world where those words do not correspond to any reality.[7] In her essay "The Use of the Beautiful" (1966), Raine observes that, since positivism and social realism dominate modern thought, beauty in the traditional sense has little place in the world human beings have created. There can be no anamnesis (Platonic recollection) of the order of the soul if that very order is denied. Consequently, to live in modern cities is to live the soul's exile; thus the permanent feeling of unrest, agitation, and emptiness that drives people to be, as Eliot put it, "distracted from distraction by distraction." In contrast, Raine argues that the arts exist to transmit or stir in us "the hidden order which we call 'the beautiful' . . . the active principle in any work of transforming power, summoning us to self-knowledge of the innate human norm to which we always tend, but from which we always deviate."[8] So Raine was heir to Blake in the "Mental Fight" against post-Enlightenment biases, to rebuild the Jerusalem of a unitary spiritual vision of nature and culture.[9] Her seven-decades-long writing career as well as the founding of the journal *Temenos* and the Temenos Academy in her old age were entirely dedicated to this project.

In this essay I propose four aspects of Raine's approach that enabled her to give form to this vision: her repeated experience and expression of self-emptying or selflessness, which is a prerequisite for contemplative insight and inspiration; the journey-myth of the generated soul, which runs through her work from start to finish; her simultaneously traditional and heterodox perspective; and the (rarely mentioned) pragmatic and earthy quality that often appears in her writings.

The beginning of Raine's first poetry collection, *Stone and Flower* (1943), announces the standpoint of her most characteristic poetry: "Sea,

---

7. Raine, "Premises and Poetry," in *Inner Journey of the Poet*, 14–24.

8. Raine, "The Use of the Beautiful," in *Defending Ancient Springs*, 156–75 (167–68).

9. The allusion here of course is to Blake's famous lyric in his preface to *Milton*, "And did those feet in ancient time . . ." Blake quotes the Book of Numbers on prophecy, which I mention at the start of this essay, immediately after this poem.

tree, and bird was I." Isolated, such a statement could be taken as mere words, a claim of mind-body unity that is only theoretical. But in the context of the whole poem, it is clear that the poet is writing from intuitive experience. Since "Lyric" is short I will quote it in full:

> A bird sings on a matin tree
> "Once such a bird was I."
>
> The sky's gaze says
> "Remember your mother."
>
> Seas, trees and voices cry
> "Nature is your nature."
>
> I reply
> "I am what is not what it was."
> Seas, trees, and bird, alas!
> Sea, tree, and bird was I.[10]

The poem opens with images of the terrestrial paradise, recollected. A bird on a tree—"matin" because it is morning but also because the time is matins, the dawn of sacred time—recollects its own archetypal birdness. The sky recalls a Demeter-mother who has been left behind. All of nature tells the "I" of the poem that virgin or Edenic nature is what that "I" truly is. And the "I"—the "I" as such, not aligned with any individual per se—acknowledges that it is "what is not what it was," the *sat-chit-ānanda* or being-consciousness-bliss of primordial creation. While the penultimate line *invokes* seas, trees, and the bird, in the last line the "I" of the poem *identifies* with them in a prelapsarian dimension. One of Raine's favorite sources, Plotinus, anticipates Raine's insight: "All beings are beings through *The One*, both such as are primarily beings, and such as in any respect whatever are said to be classed in the order of beings. For what would they be, if they were not the one? For if deprived of unity, *they are no longer that which they were said to be.*"[11]

In terms of the poem's rhythm, by which *felt* meaning is communicated in poetry, the first two lines create the expectation of standard ballad meter (a four-beat line followed by a three-beat line). Raine says in her autobiography that the ballad form was always dear to her; her Scottish

---

10. Unless otherwise stated, all quotations from Raine's poetry come from *Collected Poems*. Poems not reprinted in the *Collected* will be mentioned as such.

11. Plotinus, *Enneads* VI.ix, translated by Thomas Taylor, 397; my italics.

mother and relatives knew many traditional ballads by heart and often re-
cited them. But the second couplet interrupts the ballad-ghost, changing
to two-beat lines; the third couplet returns to the four-three pattern; and
the final stanza is composed of a dimeter line followed by three tetrameters
(four-beat lines). The result is a ballad of the Self that mimics the Self's or-
ganic and unpredictable movement. In a blurb used for Raine's early books,
Edwin Muir wrote that her poetry was "pure as from a well-spring, [with
a] fresh natural beauty undecorated and undefaced by influence." Its asym-
metry complements the living nature that Raine's poetry invokes. Indeed,
the forms of her poems are more like bark on a tree or patterns on the
surface of water than Apollonian statuary or Christopher Wren's cathedral.
This is what some reviewers have called the feminine quality of her verses.
It is consistent with the ideas of romantic predecessors such as Coleridge,
who thought of form as organic and innate, like the germ of a plant that
comes into being from inside out. In an interview, Raine commented on
her experience of the genesis of poetic form: "The form in which a poem
comes is a living form . . . born from the Imagination."[12]

Raine mentioned in various essays the special value of a few poems of
hers that seemed to compose themselves, and I imagine that this was one of
them: a holistic premonition of her life's work. All her poetry, as well as her
years of scholarly research and writing, is contained in it in seed form. Es-
sential to her perspective, as also to Blake's and Plotinus's and that of Raine's
beloved Advaita Vedānta, is the notion that matter has no independent
existence apart from mind—where "mind" obviously means a great deal
more than ratiocination or conscious thought. Mind or Spirit ("God"), not
matter, is the fundamental ontological reality. *Blake and Tradition* (1969),
as well as Raine's shorter Blake and Yeats studies, raises this point time and
again. The radical dualism of post-Cartesian thought, she asserts, has to
be countered with an even more radical nonduality.[13] Raine's vision of the

12. Interview with Brian Keeble, 29–30.

13. See for example Raine, "Yeats and Kabir," in *Yeats the Initiate*, 331–58. In this
essay Raine traces imagery in Yeats's great poem "Among Schoolchildren" to nondualist
Indian thought and the image of the chestnut tree at the end to Kabir. On Yeats's ending
the poem, "O chestnut-tree, . . . / Are you the leaf, the blossom or the bole? / O body
swayed to music, O brightening glance, / How can we know the dancer from the dance,"
Raine comments: "There is nothing in the Greek or the Christian—Western—imagery
hitherto employed to prepare us for this image of the tree. Have we not here a transition
from Platonic to Vedantic thought? I believe that the image of the chestnut-tree marks
such a transition—tree and dancer alike come from India, where the resolution of the
paradox of body and soul is to be discovered in a thousand forms" (347).

spiritual essence of a hyacinth, which she describes in her autobiography and which she mentions in her writing on several occasions, is such an experience; for example these lines from the "Uncollected" section of her *Collected Poems* (2000):

> A hyacinth in a glass it was, on my working-table,
> Before my eyes opened beyond beauty light's pure living flow.
> "It is I," I knew, "I am that flower, that light is I,
> Both seer and sight." ("To the Sun")

More often than not, it seems, critics have misunderstood the implications of this sort of thought in Raine's work, dismissing it with labels which for them are pejorative, such as "mystical" or "otherworldly" or "Platonic." They think her visionary, metaphysical perspective is a denial or minimization of the "real world" of the senses. But this is far from what Raine or her mentors believed or practiced. None of them intend a diminishment or dismissal of matter and material existence. On the contrary, they would say that matter is degraded when its subsistence in mind or consciousness is neglected. Plotinus, Blake, and Raine understood that eternity is either here and now or never and nowhere. The modernist worldview is dualistic—mind and body are separate; the world is "out there" and our faculties are "in here" and in pieces. Blake expressed the nondualist view in *Gates of Paradise:* "The Sun's Light when he unfolds it / Depends on the Organ that beholds it."[14] This is what Raine experienced with the hyacinth: seeing *through* not *with* her eyes, as Blake put it.

She was not a myth maker, as were her mentors Yeats and (especially) Blake. Raine generally expressed metaphysical themes and the story of the soul through intuitive associations between nature and the spiritual world. Raine discovered her passion and love for nature, as she writes in the first volume of her autobiography, *Farewell Happy Fields* (1973), through her Scottish mother and relatives and her early years in Northumberland. The experience of that traditional culture, in harmony with its rich natural setting, impressed her with an Edenic image that was her touchstone for life. Of her poet-mentors, Shelley is closest to Raine in his use of symbolism. As Raine writes about Shelley in her introduction to a volume of his poetry: "His symbols are not, as in Blake, as sometimes in Yeats, 'arbitrary, harsh, and difficult'; they are gathered up with the speed of thought from

---

14. K. 760.

the natural world which was for him the mirror in which he saw reflected the spiritual forms of an intelligible order."[15] So, Shelley's West Wind is also the Spirit that bloweth where it listeth; and when Shelley depicts the sky mirrored in a pool of water he is also alluding to heaven as reflected on earth or to eternity as it appears in the temporal dimension.

The theme of self-emptying or egolessness is suggested in both of the Raine poems quoted above. It is a frequent motif in her poems, a prelude or accompaniment to their visionary content, and it is related, in Raine's poetic thought, to space and time as inward realities. In her Blake writings, Raine reflects on the so-called *punctum*, which Blake opposed to the Newtonian concept of empty space and extension. For Blake, modern science's view of human insignificance in the immensity of space—the "soul shudd'ring vacuum" of the Newtonian universe—paralyzes us into spiritual passivity. Raine echoes Blake when she states in her essay "Nature and Meaning" (1986): "We cannot love what does not possess life, . . . we must rediscover that we participate in a living universe, or perish by and with our machines."[16] Or as Blake writes, in words often quoted by Raine: "Think of a white cloud as being holy, you cannot love it; but think of a holy man within the cloud, love springs up in your thoughts, for to think of holiness distinct from man is impossible to the affections. Thought alone can make monsters, but the affections cannot." And, more aphoristically: "Cloud, meteor and star / Are men seen afar."[17] In other words, the universe in its essential reality is suffused by life, mercy, and intelligibility, or God, not mechanistic soullessness. The universe as an object separate from mind does not exist. This of course is not to claim that its existence is contingent upon human observers or minds, but, rather, that its essence resides in Intellect-Being or necessary Being: God.

The understanding that space is in the mind, not the mind in space, is behind the traditional conception of the sky as an image of the heavens. *In divinis*, within the divine Principle, all points in space are together and here, just as all moments of time are simultaneous and now. As Raine writes in one of her several books on Blake:

15. Raine, introduction to Shelley, *Shelley*, 16.

16. Raine, "Nature and Meaning," in *Underlying Order*, 17–31 (30). The Blake quotation is from *The First Book of Urizen*, K. 222.

17. From *Annotations to Swedenborg's Divine Love*, K. 90; *Letter to Thomas Butts* (October 2, 1800), K. 805.

> For Blake flowers, worm, and fly are symbols both of the sig-
> nificance of even the smallest living creature and of the punctum
> itself, alike present in the least and in the greatest. The Newtonian-
> Lockean visions of magnitude, with all their implications of power
> and intimidation, meant nothing to Blake; neither is there, in his
> imagery of the minute, any trace of the sentimentalism of false
> humility, which is but the other side of the exaltation of vastness
> and power. The punctum is neither great nor small, but infinite;
> and the dignity it implies in every living essence is not relative but
> absolute. The divine life is in all not partially but totally.[18]

Accordingly, for both Blake and the German mystic Jacob Boehme, the
rainbow is a symbol of the opening of the eternal world into manifesta-
tion—as we find too in the biblical story of Noah. Likewise, the spring of
the four rivers in Eden, as the paradisiacal locus of the punctum, is to be
found nowhere and everywhere. Blake associates the images of wild thyme
(with a pun on "time") and the lark in terms of the creative *fiat*. As Raine
describes it: "From the hidden moment there springs a fountain and there
grows the wild thyme, and there the lark of inspiration builds his nest. It
is here that eternity flows into time."[19] In *Milton*, Blake writes that flowers
and their perfume are, precisely, an opening center through which infin-
ity manifests.[20] The English Platonist Thomas Taylor, whom Blake met,
expresses this idea in mythological-philosophical terms, where the Greek
goddess Rhea is the fontal divinity "through whose punctum existence
flows from nonbeing into being."[21]

The punctum is often expressed in Raine's poetry in terms of the
emptying of the individual self. The latter is an experience—a gift and a
burden—to which she was especially prone. The idea of spiritual poverty
is common to all spiritual traditions: one must become nothing to be filled
by Plenitude. To become someone spiritually is to be no one in the world's
eyes. This is true for all seekers, regardless of gender. On the other hand,
it is interesting to note that Raine's male mentors did not write about this
experience so directly or so frequently. It is hard to imagine either Blake or
Yeats writing with the same kind of vulnerable emptiness that we witness in
the poem "Lyric," quoted earlier. Perhaps it is an experience a woman would

18. Raine, *Blake and Tradition*, 2: 165–66.

19. Raine, *Blake and Tradition*, 2: 159.

20. Blake, *Milton* 31; K. 520, 46–60.

21. Quoted in Raine, *Blake and Tradition*, 2: 159. See Raine's long essay on Taylor,
including his connection to Blake, in "Thomas Taylor in England."

be especially, though not exclusively, prone to, being a kind of womb-void for the creative imagination. Whatever the case may be, Raine often found her inspiration there, as in "The Poet Answers the Accuser," from her late collection *The Oval Portrait* (1977):

> No matter what I am, . . .
> It is not I who see, who hear, who tell, but all
> Those cloud-born drops the scattering wind has blown
> To be regathered in the stream of ocean,
> The many in the one;
> For these I am,
> Water, wind and stone I am, . . .
> A note struck by the stars I am,
> A memory-trace of sun and moon and moving waters,
> A voice of the unnumbered dead, fleeting as they—
> What matter who I am?

She wrote more than one poem answering this "Accuser," the voice of doubt or disapproval, which many women say they have struggled to overcome in their extrafamilial creative or work lives. Raine would be the last to justify or explain her poetry in terms of contemporary feminist thought, for which generally she had little regard. At the same time, as she writes in her autobiography: "I have vacillated continually and suffered endlessly from the sense of guilt incurred by the conflicts between my undone or ill-done human duties and my poetic compulsions."[22] It is hard to imagine a male poet (at least one of her generation) having the same degree of conflict about such things. It may be that the unusual, quasi-preternatural capacity of Raine to experience emptiness creatively, without caving in to despair, was spurred by the tension of unresolvable personal conflict that she describes here. Poetry itself is her necessary touchstone of connection to what lies on the other side of the emptiness, her elusive spiritual home, as in "Winter Night," from *The Presence* (1987):

> So tenuous and diffuse,
> I no longer know myself
> But through the momentary sense
> Of what is present as I write.[23]

---

22. Raine, *India Seen Afar*, 26.

23. Not included in *Collected Poems*.

In this passage, the poet is in a friend's house during a storm that has knocked out the electric current. A weak candle flame in her room is a counterpart to her flickering and tenuous sense of self.

A central theme of the sequence *On a Deserted Shore* (1973) is the annihilation of self that has been brought about by Raine's loss of the Platonic lover whom she felt to be her soul mate, the naturalist-author Gavin Maxwell. The sequence opens: "Where my treasure is / A grave: / My heart also / Empty." An essay could be written about *On a Deserted Shore* as a feminine *Vita nova*, the youthful work of Dante in which his heart is broken open, first, by Beatrice's inaccessibility, and second, by her death. Grief takes the form of painful recollection of the emptiness of self apart from the beloved; individual existence is recognized as an illusion. Raine expresses this emptiness unforgettably in her poem "Self," from *The Pythoness* (1949):

> Who am I, who
> Speaks from the dust,
> Who looks from the clay?
>
> Who hears
> For the mute stone,
> For fragile water feels
> With finger and bone? . . .
>
> . . .
>
> Who out of nothingness has gazed
> On the beloved face?

Such vulnerability and emptiness result, especially in Raine's earlier volumes, in some poems that seem to arise from the transpersonal ground of being:

> A hundred years I slept beneath a thorn
> Until the tree was root and branches of my thought,
> Until white petals blossomed in my crown.
>
> A thousand years I floated in a lake
> Until my brimful eye could hold
> The scattered moonlight and the burning cloud.
>
> . . .
>
> I have raised temples of snow, castles of sand
> And left them empty as a dead hand. ("The Traveller," in *The Pythoness*)

Characteristically, the poet's identification with nature blurs the boundaries between mind and matter, inner and outer. The "I" that speaks this poem is immersed in the processes of creation, inseparable from the articulations of nature itself. It is as if no empirical self composed the poem. The poet is absent, only the eternal creative present exists, expressed in a voice that is authentically, even uncannily oracular.

Although Raine's poetry often uses striking and highly detailed natural imagery, it is (with the exception of some late poems, discussed below) rarely "naturalistic" per se. The rapid leaps between images and the use of abstract or Latinate terms, as well as the light step of her cadences, evoke a sense of the metaphysical transparency of things. In this passage from "'There Shall be no More Sea,'" collected in *The Lost Country* (1971), the poet evokes the coming together of ocean water and light, as simultaneously external phenomena and inward, visionary experience:

> . . . the heavy streaming windbeaten waves
> Consubstantial with glint and gold-dazzle flashed from glassy crests.
> On turbulence of light we float.
>
> Why then should I not walk on water? . . .
> . . .
> This body solid and visible to sense
> Insubstantial as the shouting host of the changeable wind.

Her use of "host" is reminiscent of Yeats's rushing elementals, the Orphic divinities of nature. In a poem such as "Eileann Chanaidh," from *The Hollow Hill* (1965), visual and tactile details from Canna island in the Hebrides evoke how "Home is an image written in the soul":

> And high the cliffs in eagle heart exult,
> And warm the brown sea-wrack to the seals,
> And lichened rocks grey in the buzzard's eye.

The poem "Rose," also in *The Hollow Hill*, opens with an echo of the classical *carpe diem* motif, in Robert Herrick's famous formulation, but immediately makes clear that a literal fresh or wilting rose is not the point:

> Gather while you may
> Vapour of water, dust of earth, rose
> Of air and water and light that comes and goes:
> Over and over again the rose is woven.

The archetypal Form of the rose in the eternally regenerative present is the source of the freshness that the poet of sensual existence unconsciously desires, since

> the perfect form is moving
> Through time, the rose is a transit, a wave that weaves
> Water.

In her great "Northumbrian Sequence," which opens *The Year One* (1952), Raine speaks like the Welsh bard Taliesin, from the Self that is the All, or like her contemporary Vernon Watkins, seeing through the eye socket of creation. Northumbria was Raine's Eden, her symbolic landscape of the soul's radical innocence and infant joy. Once again, the "I" of the narrator is not the poet's ego but the inspired imagination-intellect speaking the language of sacred analogy, where all of creation is a "signature" of the intelligible. Nothing is temporal, everything is simultaneous: "I was," symbolically, means "I am":

> Pure I was before the world began,
> I was the violence of wind and wave,
> I was the bird before bird ever sang.

The "I" becomes an "eye" through which *natura naturans* (nature as inwardness and archetype, as opposed to *natura naturata*, or nature as external form) inspires its human vessel, the poet:

> The sleeper at the rowan's foot
> Dreams the darkness at the root,
> Dreams the flow that ascends the vein
> And fills with world the dreamer's brain.

In *The Lion's Mouth* (1977), the third volume of her autobiography, Raine describes the waking dream or vision behind "Northumbrian Sequence":

> [I saw] the Tree, though it stood in inner space, not in nature. Maytree or Rowan, it bore its clusters of white flowers. In it was a blackbird and at the foot the sleeping figure of a young boy of about twelve years old. The tree was on the summit of a hill, and I was aware of the flow of waters into its roots, gathered from the darkness and cold storms I knew to be raging below. The tree itself, the laden branches, the singing of the bird and the flow of life from chaos and cold to form and flower and fruit was all, I knew, taking place in the mind of the sleeper; all was his thought, his dream raising the tree and its flowers continually into being.... It seemed

> an anamnesis of the soul's native place, the immortal world, the
> reality within and beyond appearances, the same that I had seen
> in the hyacinth.

This "anamnesis" is poetic inspiration itself, "the awakening of imaginative recollection, the true poetic initiation, which is the soul's remembering not of its mortal but of its immortal history; not of individual knowledge but of the one consciousness."[24] As Raine puts it in another poem in *The Year One*, in contemplation, the self becomes "An eye only, one of the eyes of earth" ("Seventh Day"). This is reminiscent of Emerson's famous metaphor of the walking eyeball, transparent to nature.

The line between seer and seen is blurred; the "I" of the poems is never just an observer, but is a participant in the creative matrix. The poem "Spell of Creation," also in *The Year One*, begins with "an eye" in a "ring of iron." A transformation occurs by which the ring becomes an "O" that is the "eye" inside which "swims a sea," which in turn contains the sky's reflection and the sun, and then a "bird of gold." The latter is the second metamorphosis in the poem, for in the bird there is "a heart" from which "flows a song," inside which there is a "word" that "speaks a world." The word is the Logos, the Son, through whom, says the Nicene Creed, all things are made, including the poem's "I" or "eye."

In a few passages, Raine's oracular voice is more unadorned and exposed; the symbolic language of nature is minimized, leaving only the austere beauty of being itself. Who, for example, is the speaker of "Message," from *The Year One*, here quoted in its entirety?

> Look, beloved child, into my eyes, see there
> Your self, mirrored in that living water
> From whose deep pools all images of earth are born.
> See, in the gaze that holds you dear
> All that you were, are, and shall be for ever.
> In recognition beyond time and seeming
> Love knows the face that each soul turns towards heaven.

This poem's central motif or image is the voice that utters it. True identity is united with the "deep pools [from which] all images of earth are born." With characteristically simple, direct language and delicate cadences, Raine shares a visionary recital of being in the eternal present. Brian Keeble has referred to this as the "undivided presence" in Raine's early poems, whose

---

24. Raine, *Autobiographies*, 270–73.

images are especially lived and inhabited, while in the later poems there is more of a distance between the poet-speaker and the poem's content.[25]

Much of Raine's poetry oscillates between the experience of self-emptying and poetic inspiration, which I have been describing, and nostalgic suffering over the memory of that freedom from the perspective of selfhood and ego-identity. In "Three Poems of Incarnation," for example, from *The Year One*, the poet is aware of a great divide between her childhood experience of bliss in nature and her present worldly self, where "All that I have come to be / Lies between my heart and the rose." This sense of being in a "fallen" state increases in Raine's next collection, *The Hollow Hill*, which was published thirteen years after *The Year One*, during which time she was deeply immersed in her Blake studies. Where the earlier collection had opened with the great release from self evoked in "Northumberland Sequence," this volume starts with "Night Thought," a poem that clearly draws on Raine's research into Blake's myth of the soul's descent. "Night Thought" is followed by a poem that addresses this directly:

> A cloud unspeakably troubled
> Dims the light and cries with voice inarticulate,
> A cloud of woman drawn up from the bitter sea.
>
> I, I darken that which is all eye,
> Hide in a shroud of blood the soul's dead face.
> ("'A Certain Moist Nature . . .'")

It is not surprising that this latter poem, whose title is a quotation from the *Hermetica*, was *not* included in Raine's *Collected Poems*; it is too derivative of Blake and it expresses a theme that comes up elsewhere with greater subtlety. Another sign of Blake's influence, appearing throughout *The Hollow Hill*, is Raine's adoption of the longer line, which she handles gracefully but which, one feels, is not the poet's most natural medium. Shorter lines (two to four beats) generally work better for her remarkable darting intuition, while her longer lines tend to be prosier, sometimes to the point of being indistinguishable from prose. As the cover flap of the first edition of *The Year One* stated: "Poetry, for Miss Raine, is rather a mode of thought than a technical exercise; and this is both the strength and the weakness of her verse." The shorter lines, which work so well in her late meditative sequences, express rapid brushstrokes of thought.

25. Keeble, *Kathleen Raine*, 9.

References to the loss of Edenic oneness appear throughout Raine's writing. In her late poem "A Departure," collected in *The Presence*, she says that "Eternity's long now is for us unending departure." The theme of this poem is the interpenetration of past, present, and future, and the relation of these to the ageless self, which nevertheless constantly undergoes change and death.

As Raine intuited when she was young, and learned to formulate in great detail from Blake, Thomas Taylor, and others, human beings in the state of empirical selfhood easily forget that phenomena (including the quotidian self) are contingent and relative. Phenomena only *participate* in being without having any claim to it per se. And such forgetting is spiritual death, since it is blind to the true nature of things. As Plato states in *Gorgias*, cited by Porphyry in his discussion of the World Cave: "Who knows whether to live is not to die, and to die is not to live"; and as Socrates puts it, in life perhaps we are actually dead in a spiritual sense.[26]

Raine's groundbreaking essay on Blake's painting *The Sea of Time and Space* demonstrates how its imagery draws on Porphyry's myth of the World Cave.[27] This richly symbolic picture alludes to the process of generation through the weaving nymphs and the descent through the Northern tropic of Capricorn, while the ascent back to the world of the immortals takes place through the Southern gate of Cancer. For Blake, the generated soul has fallen into a deadly sleep. To be born is to enter a cave which is also a grave, which in turn is the body woven like a garment by the feminine deities. For the Neoplatonists, matter is nonentity, pure potential lacking in form except to the degree that it reflects the intelligible essences. The soul's descent into time and matter is a death from eternity.

Raine expresses the pain and exhilaration of this in "Three Poems of Incarnation," from *The Year One:*

> There came a boat riding the storm of blood
> And in the boat a child,
>
> In the boat a child
> Riding the waves of song,
> Riding the waves of pain.

This boy is the *puer aeternus* (eternal boy), who, note, rides the waves of pain as well as song: "I am your child, in darkness and fear / On the verge

---

26. Quoted in Raine, *Blake and Tradition*, 1: 96.

27. This essay is chapter 3 of volume 1 of *Blake and Tradition.*

of being," he says. This child clearly is associated with Blake's Thel, as well as the other figures, discussed by Raine, whom Blake used in addressing the themes of the generation of the soul and the constraints of corporeal life on the spirit:

> Go back, my child, to the rain and the storm
> For in this house there is sorrow and pain
> In the lonely night.

Like Christ or the bodhisattvas but unlike Thel, the child chooses to share with other sentient beings the trials and illusions of incarnate existence, *saṃsāra*:

> I will not go back for hate or sin,
> I will not go back for sorrow or pain,
> For my true love mourns within
> On the threshold of night.

Raine's strong bond with her mother, which she evokes many times in her writings, translates into her identification with the myth of the Kore, or Persephone, who is ravished by Hades and stolen from the idyllic and flourishing world she shared with her mother, Demeter. Blake expresses this motif in a number of feminine figures—Lyca, Thel, Vala, Oothoon, and others—through whom he represents the soul's generation. It seems that Raine sees herself in these imaginal figures, each in a different way: "Oothoon is the noblest of the three: Thel fears to descend; Lyca falls asleep; but Oothoon brings into the cave the memories and values of eternity. Because she possesses this knowledge she knows that physical forms are embodiments of spiritual essences."[28] The title of the second volume of Raine's autobiography, *The Land Unknown* (1975), is taken from Blake's poem *Thel*. This is the installment of Raine's memoir in which she tells of the loss of the Edenic world of Northumberland, before her fall into the positivist atmosphere at Cambridge, two unhappy marriages, and various other descents of the soul. Raine never had much money; she stayed true to her vocation by stealth and grace throughout the turbulent events of her life. As I mentioned, this down-to-earth aspect of Raine may come to a surprise to critics who have not really absorbed her work. She was a visionary with her feet on the ground.

---

28. Raine, *Blake and Tradition*, 1: 166.

Blake writes in his annotations to Johann Kaspar Lavater's *Aphorisms on Man*: "God is in the lowest effects as well as in the highest causes"[29]—and so he posits a single principle operating through contraries. Ultimately, Raine finds more affinity with Blake's view of the descent of the soul than with that of the Neoplatonists. Like Blake, she vacillates between the Neoplatonic understanding, which sees an unbridgeable chasm between the spiritual home and incarnate existence, and the alchemical nondualist *coincidentia oppositorum* and transformation of matter. Where the Neoplatonists, figured in Blake by world-denying Thel, focus on the loss that the soul undergoes when it descends into the world of appearances, alchemists such as Boehme and Paracelsus prefer the wholeness captured in the *Emerald Tablet*'s famous dictum, "As above so below." For them, and for Blake in *The Marriage of Heaven and Hell* and in many passages in his prophetic books, all of being, including the outer world, is a unity within mind or consciousness. Thel had failed to grasp that "the soul is not transient in the world, but the world is transient in the soul."[30] Raine chooses this nondualist solution herself; we see this, for example, in her late poetry, where she turns to personal subject matter, most memorably in the heartfelt poems about her mother in *The Oval Portrait*.

Obviously, neither Blake nor Raine ever recommend literalism, or materialism, as an end in itself. Both unwaveringly believe that the true human being is the Spirit, the Intellect—"Jesus the Imagination." The babe in *Songs of Experience* struggles against its swaddling-bands, and elsewhere in Blake, Rahab and Tirzah bind down the sons of Albion on the "stems of vegetation" with cruel fingers, and man's eternal mind is bound in the cave of the body at the bidding of Urizen. Likewise, as we have seen, Raine often expresses the soul's generated state as one of painful separation and longing. Even admitting the alchemical teaching of the transmutation of matter through spiritual activity, a bedrock notion which neither Raine nor Blake ever abandon is that the "sickness of Albion," or of the modernist soul, stems from the belief that phenomena possess substantial existence independent of mind. For Raine, this catastrophic error is a virus, as it were, spreading its sickness, the illness of the *anima mundi* or soul of the world, which manifests in the global environmental crisis. She believes that "matter" suffers just as much as "soul" does when we deny that the principle of manifestation must itself be unmanifest and spiritual, and world-denying

29. K. 87.

30. Raine, *Blake and Tradition*, 1: 181.

spirituality is only another way of tormenting an already sick patient. She and her mentors understand "life" as Imagination or Intellect-Being—neither abstraction nor mindless sensation. All our "sensuous" experience is a perpetual *vision* of what Blake calls the "Sons of Los," or the living imagination. The imagination reanimates the soul of things—or rather, *is* that living soul, because it is a return to the font of consciousness. This *living* knowledge is the sap of the universe. In her later years, Raine found confirmation of her fidelity to the middle way of the *mundus imaginalis* (imaginal world) in the writings of the scholar of Islamic mysticism Henry Corbin. Through Corbin, she elaborated and reinforced the metaphysical basis she had learned from Blake, of the imagination as the realm that mediates between matter and pure spirit-intellect. The imagination reveals the essential *unity* of matter and spirit. The right question to ask about the Earth, says Corbin, is not *what* it is but *who* it may be, "*who* are the waters, plants, mountains, or *to whom* do they correspond?"[31] In this view, the modernist abuse of nature arises from a profound failure of imagination. So, from Raine's perspective, just as Blake's "dark Satanic Mills" were a state of mind as well as an external reality of industrializing England, the dying coral reefs are within us. Likewise the enormous islands of trash floating in the oceans and the albatrosses dying from the plastic they have ingested on their remote islands. Whales have been found dead with up to eighty-eight pounds of plastic in their bodies. Global climate change caused by the carbon dioxide emissions associated with fossil fuel combustion has resulted in ever more frequent extreme weather patterns, fires, and floods. Scientists assembled by the United Nations in 2019 reported that a million species, a *quarter* of the plant and animal species on earth, are endangered with extinction due to relentless pursuit of economic growth. This is the world re-created in the image of rational empiricism's dead universe—a reification of our mental state.

A SUPERFICIAL CRITIQUE OF Raine's work might view her "confessional" poems, especially prominent in her later collections, as a departure from her visionary work. But from the nondualist point of view that Raine cultivated, *māyā* too is an aspect of reality; the most fleeting of things is present to being and to that extent eternally *is*:

31. Raine's translation from Corbin's *Corps spirituelle et terre celeste* (Spiritual Body and Celestial Earth), in "Towards a Living Universe," in *Inner Journey of the Poet*, 207.

The sun that rose
From the sea this morning
Will never return, . . .

. . .

Never this sun,
This world, and never
Again this watcher. ("The Moment," from *The Year One*)

That very "never-again-ness" is a trace of the eternal present, so "Earth's story must all be told, nothing left out" ("The Eighth Sphere," in *The Hollow Hill*). Raine's unprogrammatic approach increased in her writings throughout her lengthy old age. Her passionate love for India and her many visits there reinforced this commitment. She loved Indian culture's pragmatism, spirituality, and unsentimental openness to vital energies, and she aimed for a similar attitude in her own life and writing.[32]

The Oval Portrait was a watershed volume in this regard. It contains poems about Raine's encroaching sense of mortality, without resorting to spiritual consolations or metaphysics or even myth: just the ordinary heartbreak of loss. The title poem, about Raine's mother Jessie Wilkie, written shortly after her death, is moving for its simplicity and directness:

At eighteen, you stood for this faded photograph,
Your young hand awkwardly holding the long skirt
Over that light foot no trammelling at your heels could stay . . .

. . .

Those young eyes, unfaded by your ninety years
Still saw in each day earth's wonders new-begun.

Such personal and intimate recollections continue in Raine's later volumes; for example, in "My Mother's Birthday" from *The Oracle in the Heart* (1980):

I used to watch you, sleeping,
Your once brown shining ringlets gray.
It was your way to lie,
Your knees high, your old twisted hands
In the archaic posture of the unborn . . .

. . .

Why had not your mother, bending over her baby,
Ninety years ago, wrapped you warm?
I, your daughter, felt pity
For that unwanted babe, for comfort too long ago, too far away.

32. See the fourth volume of her autobiography, *India Seen Afar*.

The plain style of this lovely passage fits the humble subject and makes it more tangible and immediate. Although these poems do not have the scope or reach of her visionary work, they communicate a warm humanity that "leaves nothing out."

It is rather wonderful that the elderly Raine, in such pieces, let go of what she and her readers had come to expect of her poetry, and just wrote from the heart. She never was one for rules for their own sake—her commitment to the imagination would not allow it. There is, however, a persistent note even in these poems that runs through nearly all her poetry: the sense that life in this world is a form of exile from the heart's true home—from infinite Life. As she writes about her father, in a poem from the "Uncollected" section of her *Collected Poems*:

> His month was windy March, when coltsfoot flowers
> Open their bright disks to receive the sun, or close
> Against the chill and cloud of a harsh season.
> On my childhood my father shone like an early sun,
> Who in his old age closed his rays against the cold
> Climate of a loveless house. ("My Father's Birthday")

Passages such as these belie Raine's criticisms of "self-expression" in contemporary poetry. These confessional pieces are instances of what she herself referred to as poetry that "comes from the world of feeling, of the individual soul"[33]—less singular, certainly, than her visionary poems, but nevertheless essential to her overall body of work. What she really was criticizing, perhaps, was *complacent* self-expression that looks no further, forgetting or dismissing its wider context.

Another very late poem, "Garden Simurgh," accepts things as they are even in the dirty literal city, London, where sparrows, not Sufi wonderbirds, are to be found.[34] In any case, the poet asks, how are the magical birds of sacred fable

> more miraculous
> Than these two-a-farthing sparrows

33. Raine, "Poetry as Prophecy," in *Yeats and Learning of the Imagination*, 101.

34. The "Simurgh" is a name from the medieval Persian narrative *The Conference of the Birds*, by the Sufi Attar, which chronicles the journey of the world's birds as they seek their sovereign lord, the mythical Simurgh. The flock of thousands of birds must cross several treacherous valleys to reach Simurgh's mountain. Thirty survive, and only upon arrival do they realize that they themselves, in fact, *are* the Simurgh. *Simurgh* in Persian means thirty (*si*) birds (*murgh*). Their search all along has been to find themselves.

Each feather bearing the carelessly-worn signature
Of the universe that has brought them here to the Lord's table
With such delight, never doubting their welcome?

Similarly, the opening lines of a late untitled poem state:

I believe nothing—what need
Surrounded as I am with marvels of what is,
This familiar room, books, shabby carpet on the floor . . .
. . .
This inexhaustible, untidy world—
I would not have it otherwise.

This is part and parcel of her commitment to lived reality: acceptance
brings its own blessings. Having earned this wisdom, she could write in
another late piece, "Short Poems 1994":

Against the nihil
One candle-flame, one blade of grass,
One thought suffices
To affirm all.

In Raine's advanced old age, she often stated that she had come to
realize that all knowledge is ultimately straw, that the point is to reside
mindfully with one's whole being in the mystery of things as they reveal
themselves. While she never stopped drawing on the perennial philosophy
and criticizing the rootlessness and materialism of the modern world, she
was quite explicit in her dislike of dogmatic or rigid traditionalism. Ironi-
cally, much of her reason for doing so was consistent with Traditionalist
thought itself, which never confuses inspired intuition with rote doctrinaire
formulations.[35] And there is no doubt that the Traditionalists, especially
A. K. Coomaraswamy, were a key source for Raine's efforts to revive the sa-
cred in art and poetry. She agreed with the medieval dictum, often repeated
by Coomaraswamy, that *ars sine scientia nihil est*, art is nothing without
knowledge. For Seyyed Hossein Nasr, although Raine was not "completely
rooted in traditional metaphysics . . . she realized the significance of tradi-
tional doctrines."[36] She agreed with Guénon's and others' criticism of the
modern world as being essentially antitraditional and full of almost

35. I am using the capitalized word *Traditionalist* here in reference to the school of
thought whose leading figures are René Guénon, A. K. Coomaraswamy, Titus Burck-
hardt, Frithjof Schuon, Seyyed Hossein Nasr, and others.

36. Nasr, "Kathleen Raine and Tradition," 183.

insurmountable obstacles to those who resist the reign of quantity and dogmatic scientism. And yet, as Nasr points out, she did seem to value artworks of genius on a par with the revelations of orthodoxy—while for Traditionalists, "a single page of a *Purāṇa* is worth all the writings of Tagore."[37] Raine often seems to have had more faith in prophecy and imagination than in traditional forms. In this, she was like her mentors, especially Yeats, who believed in the salvific potential of poetry in the modern age. As Yeats writes in *Ideas of Good and Evil*, in former times people "believed that they amused themselves with books of imagination, but that they 'made their souls' by listening to sermons, . . . [But] in our time we are agreed that we 'make our souls' out of some one of the great poets of ancient times," or out of more recent great authors—but make a "poorer sort of soul, by listening to sermons."[38] Yeats's comment may have been mischievously hyperbolic, but he was of course right that many sermons are boring and less spiritually nourishing than good poetry. This is not surprising, when we consider that much modern religious thought has been reduced to doctrine and ethics devoid of intellectual insight and symbolism. So Raine would certainly agree that *living* tradition in our age is often more available from the poets than from the preachers.

Nevertheless, throughout her work Raine draws on traditional wisdom as an essential touchstone and guide. She is aware that, from the standpoint of Tradition, the path of unguided inspiration is fraught with perils, particularly in an age when, as Yeats put it, "the centre cannot hold." As a perennialist, she is orthodox within her heterodoxy, arguing in her prose and embodying in her poetry the conviction that "mental things alone are real." She believes that we are at the end of a cycle—which she sometimes refers to as the late Kali Yuga but more often as the culmination of a Platonic Great Year—in which the informing spirit of the previous civilization is departing and no amount of wishful thinking or traditional doctrine is going to bring it back. Various political and religious persuasions may impose dogmatic coagulants to stop the bleeding of the old cycle, and yet the wound remains open and no approach, orthodox or otherwise, can magically stanch it. For example, the so-called "save the West" movement of the Dignitatis Humanae Institute, founded by the British conservative Benjamin Harnwell, has attempted to set up an ideological "boot camp" in

37. Coomaraswamy, "Eastern Religions and Western Thought."

38. Quoted in Raine, "Poetry as Prophecy," in *Yeats and Learning of the Imagination*, 96–97.

a monastery near Rome, led by the American far-right provocateur Steve Bannon. Such groups promote a tribalistic, intolerant, and retrograde culture and ethic, at a time of unprecedented globalization and pluralism. In response to these trends, Pope Francis has criticized hidebound traditionalists of every faith for viewing tradition as a static container. Rather, as he puts it, "Tradition is like roots [of a tree], which give us nutrition to grow. You will not become like the roots. You will flower, grow, give fruit. And the seeds become roots for other people."[39] This is an approach that resonates with Raine's. For her, tradition is not primarily transmission of the dead letter, but the abiding presence of the living spirit, which historical forms may or may not impart. So, at the end of an age, we do well to preserve and transmit traditional wisdom for its fertilizing virtues, not only for our own time but for that of the next cycle. This view in itself is "traditional," in the properly understood sense of tradition as a catalyst for awakening and embracing change. To balance tradition and modernity, the key is to be fluid and open to the unknown, while remaining rooted in principial wisdom.[40] And in fact, as we have seen, Raine puts her trust in the unknown, in the soul's dark night, even as she depends on and affirms the wisdom traditions.

On one hand, as Raine sees it, materialist thought and its mechanical universe have run their course; on the other, tradition and orthodoxy can go only so far in bringing us to the next creative phase. The rest is up to God. As she said in a paper delivered at the Eranos Conference in 1968, we are living "at a moment of cataclysmic reversal and renewal of an age, . . . [where] any statement made about 'the two cultures' which is less than mythological must seem inadequate. At such a moment of the reversal of the gyres, our relation both to tradition and to the present must have an unprecedented character."[41] It is "A time to undo, to unknow," rather than "a time / To build those cloud-capped towers," she writes in an untitled poem ("World's music changes") in *The Presence*. All of this is consistent with Raine's (and her mentors') faith that even as the outward forms of culture collapse or are overrun by ignorance and barbarism, the essential Truth survives: "whatever is of the living imagination will rise from its grave."[42]

39. Quoted in McElwee, "Francis Criticizes Traditionalist Catholics."

40. A recent, lucid discussion of this is Lakhani, *Faith and Ethics*, especially chapter 3, "Tradition and Modernity," 35–52.

41. Raine, "Poetic Symbols as a Vehicle of Tradition," in *Inner Journey of the Poet*, 47–48.

42. Raine, "Poetic Symbols as a Vehicle of Tradition," in *Inner Journey of the Poet*, 75.

This was the gist of Blake's vision of the Last Judgment, which takes place within the human soul. And as Yeats writes in his late poem "The Gyres":

> Things thought too long can be no longer thought,
> For beauty dies of beauty, worth of worth,
> And ancient lineaments are blotted out . . .
>
> . . .
>
> What matter? Out of cavern comes a voice,
> And all it knows is that one word "Rejoice!"

Likewise, Raine thought that the break-up of outward forms and the "reversal of premises" is but another way that the divine Intellect-Imagination which created those forms communicates and expresses itself. She reminds us in this connection of the triple aspect of the divine being in the Vedānta—Creator, Preserver, and Destroyer. This is the subject of her last published poem, "Millennial Hymn to the Lord Shiva" (2000):

> To whom shall we pray
> When our vision has faded
> But the world-destroyer,
> The liberator, the purifier?

She believed that the universe is a "manifestation of the ever-various energy of the divine mind that is always and everywhere its own law." This is the play of God in the Vedānta, or Blake's "sports of Wisdom," so that "'Everything that lives is holy' not because the poet chooses to think so, but because all consciousness and all impulse is from the living divine spirit. Nature has no other 'laws' . . . for the living spirit is reality itself."[43] In other words, the apparently inexorable spiritual and cultural entropy that is so palpable in our time can occur on the terrestrial plane only, not *in divinis*: "Civilizations vanish, our own is near its end, yet the undying spirit remains itself."[44] The fundamental thing, in the midst of our challenging collective moment, is to keep "the Divine Vision in time of trouble"; to resist the negative currents, as Ali Lakhani says, "through spiritual and ethical striving in an age whose very spirit is pitted against the Spirit itself."[45] Raine never falters in this charge, because her commitment is to the informing spirit of life, which cannot be lost any more than essential reality can stop

43. Raine, *Blake and Tradition*, 2: 128.

44. Raine, *India Seen Afar*, 70.

45. Blake, *Jerusalem* 95; K. 742, 20; personal communication from Ali Lakhani, May 9, 2019.

being the essentially real. So, although she does not mince words about the direness of contemporary events, she can write:

> The great tree is at this time showering down its leaves in a process of death which cannot be arrested, and whose record is everywhere to be read in the nihilism of the arts, of social life, in a thousand images of disintegration, in the reversion of civilized society, it may be, to a state of barbarism.
>
> Those who are indissolubly wedded to the external forms, whether of a religion or of a culture, must at this time despair; unable to withdraw from these what for centuries has been projected into them, they lose, when these fail, portions of their souls; but those who are able to rediscover within themselves all that has been progressively withdrawn from our dismantled world, need not fear the withdrawal of the informing presence from the beautiful forms itself created.
>
> The process of death cannot be arrested, civilizations cannot be saved; but there are the seeds, the living among the dead, who do not participate in the collective disintegration, but guard their secret of immortality, the essence of what has been and may be again. Who can say into what soil these seeds may be sown, or into what region of the universe the harvest of the world is gathered?[46]

---

46. Raine, *The Lion's Mouth*, in *Autobiographies*, 356.

"Towards This Big Objective"

A Conversation with Peter Russell

ORN IN BRISTOL, ENGLAND, *in 1921, the poet Peter Russell served*
with the British Army in India, Burma, and Malaya during World
War II. After the war, he founded and edited the journal Nine
(1949–56), one of the outstanding literary reviews of that period. The jour-
nal was known for its substantial, often trenchant reviews as well as for its
ambitious program of introducing readers to world literature through transla-
tions and essays. Russell also started Pound Press, which published books and
pamphlets by Ezra Pound and others. In 1950 he edited and introduced the
anthology An Examination of Ezra Pound, *with essays by various authors,*
which helped reactivate interest in Pound's work after a period of neglect.
From the early 1950s until 1963 Russell operated a used bookstore in Lon-
don's Soho; and from the mid-1960s until the early 1970s he lived in Venice,
where he visited with Pound regularly. In the mid- to late 1970s he taught in
British Columbia; was resident poet at Purdue University in Indiana; and was
in Teheran, where he taught at the Imperial Iranian Academy of Philosophy
at the time of the revolution of 1978–79. Russell returned to Italy after that,
living for many years in the countryside near Arezzo, where he wrote, studied,
and published prolifically until he went blind toward the end of his life. He
died in January 2003, in the Valdarno region of Tuscany, where he had been
living for more than twenty years in an isolated old mill house, La Turbina.

The following interview took place on November 14, 2000, at La Tur-
bina. A little less than halfway through the interview a third person joined us
—Lenny Emmanuel, who at the time was the poetry editor of the New Laurel
Review *in New Orleans. The few passages where the three of us are speaking*

are clearly labeled as such; other passages are just the dialogue between Russell and me. About a third of the way into the interview, while discussing Pound, the question of Pound's antisemitism came up. As a close friend and admirer of Pound, Russell plays down and oversimplifies this issue, but I have left his words intact, and have done the same with his statements about the fascist or far-right intellectuals Giovanni Gentile and Julius Evola.

My notes from that day describe my some of my first impressions of Russell.

I arrived at Peter Russell's home in Pian di Scò, in the Valdarno region south of Florence, at about eight in the morning. His house, a big converted brick mill, was located at the end of a dirt road in a grassy area where a couple of junked cars were parked, with a steepish trail leading down from there. At the bottom of the slope on which the house was perched there was a stream and a gushing falls, which I recognized from several passages in Russell's writings.

At the door, its windows laced with cobwebs and dust, Russell appeared after I'd knocked a few times. He looked his age—more so than I expected from the photographs in recent newspaper articles. He was bent over and thin, with a big mane of white hair and a beard, though still emanating force and energy. His mouth was largely hidden in facial hair, which was yellowish with nicotine. Later on in our visit, I was surprised when I noticed how small his head appeared, buried in all that hair; and also struck by how flushed and clear his skin was, despite his steady diet of whiskey and cigarettes (forty to sixty nonfilter smokes a day). His blue eyes, when they were not obscured by the thick lenses of his glasses, were penetrating and sharp.

The house itself had six rooms, all its walls discolored and needing paint. On the ground floor was the big room where you entered and then the kitchen off of that. Upstairs was the bathroom, as well as bedrooms that I didn't see. And there was a third floor, which Russell said was filled with boxes of papers, whatever survived a flood and a fire in the early 1990s. Everywhere there were papers and books. With a quick glance I saw Toynbee's Dante dictionary, Yeats's *Autobiographies*, an introduction to Sufism, and other texts. Even in the bathroom on a low table near the toilet, was an Italian edition of Góngora's sonnets, which Russell was reading at the time. I noted how organized the papers in the big downstairs room were—file trays stacked one on the other, each labeled by title or author of the photocopied article it held. On several shelves in that room there were stacks of Russell's books, many of them spiral-bound photocopies, covered with clear plastic sheets. On the kitchen table was a box stuffed with index cards that Russell kept records on. The one with my name was out, filled in with the names of the books and articles he had sent to me.

The kitchen was cluttered, and there was no running water that day. On the table where we did the interview was a plastic tablecloth, gray with various stains and cigarette ashes. There was an open bottle of Scotch on the middle of the table. I pushed aside an ashtray, juice, milk, pens, and other things to find a place for the tape recorder and my notes. Next to the chair where he had me sit was a big open barrel of trash.

A while after starting the interview, we took a break at ten o'clock or so and went to the post office and then for groceries. People in town called him *Professore.* We went to the train station eight kilometers away to meet Lenny Emmanuel. Lenny, a doctor from New Orleans who had a black hat on, was about fifty-five or sixty. We stopped at a store for lunch on the way back. Russell bought three bottles of Scotch—he drank one a day—and whole-wheat crackers. He refused my offer of a sandwich: "I don't believe in food," he quipped.

Back at his place, with lunch and whiskey and wine (Lenny bought some Montepulciano Vino Nobile), the conversation was animated, expansive, and sometimes hilarious. I have changed no words in the interview, though I did edit material to keep the written dialogue cohesive and to the point.

FRISARDI: *I thought we could start by talking about* Nine *and the literary scene at that time in London. You started* Nine *in the late forties [1949], right?*

RUSSELL: Yes, it was started two years before [1947], but then it never really got off the ground. It got into the hands of a gallery owner. He was going to put up the money and we were going to call it *Acropolis.* And Charles Tomlinson, who was then still an undergraduate at Cambridge, became a great friend at that time, and we planned it together. Then Charles moved off somewhere else in England, and I rather lost touch with him; I only saw him once or twice a year. And I collected these other friends of mine—nine of us. The most brilliant of them was D. S. Carne-Ross. Do you know his name?

I know the name, yes.

He's a classicist. A very, very clever man, but quite uncreative. He taught with [William] Arrowsmith and several other people at Texas. But we had weekly meetings, just the editors, with a few extra people, like John Heath-Stubbs, who was a good friend; David Gascoyne came sometimes, Kathleen [Raine] came sometimes.

You started Nine *after discovering Pound, right?*

Oh yes, yes.

That was the impetus for it.

Oh, yes. Pound lay behind it. But we soft-pedaled Pound, because we didn't want to offend the literary world by praising him to the skies at that time. He himself wanted it that way, too. I was in constant touch with him. I got two or three letters a week from him. Quite a lot of them are at Texas, some at Buffalo, and the rest got burned. Then there was Eliot, putting on the brake all the time. That was helpful. He would cough up cash every now and then, that was really useful [*laughs*].

What was he putting on the brakes about?

Well, about Pound and about anything that was not quite polite. We had to be very polite. For instance, I referred to Macmillan's, who had kept Thomas Hardy and Yeats out of print for many years during the war, as MacMillions, and he said, "You can't say that sort of thing," and I did, I printed it just the same.

Did he like the magazine?

Oh, yes, he liked it very much, except for those things which were sort of youthful effervescence, and I was the great villain there. I would say quite nasty things about quite important people. No doubt I did myself quite a lot of harm. But at least people found it lively.

How did the title Nine *come about?*

It was a mixture of things. The nine Muses; and also Dante's conception of the number nine as one less than perfection, or the number ten, which referred to the Empyrean. Also, there were nine of us originally in the group that started the magazine.

Who were the writers that you were publishing in Nine?

Well, there was Robert Graves, E. E. Cummings [also Pound, Eliot, Tom Scott, Allen Tate, Edith Sitwell, Wyndham Lewis, Hugh Kenner, and others], and Roy Campbell figured big in the later issues of *Nine*. Roy Campbell was the cause of the nine of us breaking up. They wouldn't accept some things that Roy wrote. Roy was reviewing the regius professor of Spanish at Cambridge—his book on Jiménez. And Roy found all sorts of really schoolboy errors—so-called misinterpretations, errors of simple language, and Roy wrote, "We don't expect poetic talent from a translator, but at least we expect accuracy." And then he translated the same poems by Jiménez, and another by Quevedo, which the regius professor [J. B. Trend]—what was his name? I can't remember—had mucked up. He just did them, like that.

I remember, Roy and I used to have lunch together in a particular pub, virtually every day, because we shared an office in Kensington, and about half past ten when it opened we'd repair to the pub, drink seven or eight or ten pints of beer, then go back to his house. We'd collect a couple of bottles of rough Spanish wine, take them back to the house, have a nibble and some wine, then Roy would lie diagonally on the floor—it was a room a bit bigger than this [Russell's not very large kitchen], no furniture, practically nothing. He would lie down on the floor with Baudelaire open on the left and a notebook in the middle, and, the first time I saw him doing this, I thought he was copying it. He wasn't: he was translating it, at the speed that you or I would copy something carefully. Amazing. He was a marvelous man, terribly amusing, and of course he, again, was very rambunctious. He was attacking everybody all the time, including his close friends.

Who were the other people connected with Nine?

Well, D. S. Carne-Ross before anybody. A man called Brian Soper, who lives in Delaware. An Englishman. Very clever man. He reminded me always of

Coleridge; he looked very like Coleridge, for a start, and he had a very slow, but sure way—without any pomposity—of talking *real good* philosophy. And he helped a lot with ideas—the cultural background. He didn't write a great deal, he's published very little. Yes, and then Iain Fletcher. A mediocre poet; quite good, I mean, if you read him now you'd think he was a jolly good poet, but in those days, when we had real poets living in England, he was rather minor. But a very scholarly man, almost a parody of the scholarly pedant. But full of good ideas. And he introduced me to things like Gnosticism, like metaphysical and baroque imagery, about which I knew nothing.

Your background up to this point was science, right?

Well, yes, I had a lot of science. None of them knew anything about science at all. Well, Soper knew a little bit, but the others didn't. And they knew very little about visual art, whereas I had traveled all over Italy, almost to every town of any size, seeing all the important paintings and sculptures.

I can see in your lyrics how a scientific vocabulary comes in with a sort of more traditional lyric vocabulary.

Yes, yes. I use words which have many faces, I use a word—I can't give you an example off the top of my mind, but a word which could be a traditional, literary, lyrical word or a philosophical word, but it also has a modern scientific ring about it. I'm not following up Empson's conception of ambiguity, as I understand it—I read Empson forty years ago, and I knew it very well. A very minor poet but with a very special touch to him. Graves I found much more . . . I mean, Graves is pretty good. His prose is awfully good too. Carcanet Press are printing the whole of Graves *and* the whole of MacDiarmid. Twenty or thirty volumes—beautiful books to handle. So I'm rereading Graves and MacDiarmid, whom I knew very well.

Now, was he [MacDiarmid] involved in Nine?

I'm wondering whether we published anything by him. Certainly I reviewed some of his books in *Nine*. But I don't know whether we published anything *by* him. You see my collaborators were very anticommunist—so was I, but in a different way. MacDiarmid was a rather absurdly loud-mouthed communist. In fact, one of those Scotsmen who are always shouting. But of course he had a fine intelligence as well. You've got to sort out the claptrap from the, you know, "We the people have no time for the bourgeois!" [*Laughs.*] We're all bourgeois. He wasn't. He lived in a little crofter's cottage with an earth floor, he had no water taps, no bath. He really lived a traditional way.

What about your correspondence with Pound at that time?

Well, see, up till '57, when he was released, he would write two to three letters to me a week—they were mainly sort of telegraphese, "Do this, do that"—always useful. Then when he came back to Italy, the correspondence didn't fade out, but I got one thing perhaps in a month or six weeks. Then I met him in Rapallo, for the first time physically—I spent two weeks with him and Olga [Rudge], near Rapallo—Sant'Ambrosio. And that was delightful. But of course he was . . . I wouldn't say finished, but he didn't talk much. He obviously . . . some of the time he didn't really know what he was doing. At any rate, we got on extremely well, as always—that would have been summer of '65. In the winter of '65 I came to live in Venice, partly because I loved Venice and partly because Ezra was frequently in Venice. So between '65 and his death in '72, I was seeing him in Venice once, twice, three times a week. Olga was a wonderful hostess, and she liked asking me always because Pound liked me—and he would talk to me. With the other people he wouldn't talk . . . All my notes were burned [in the fire in Russell's house in the early 1990s]. I kept careful notes of everything he said. I went home late at night and wrote it all down before going to sleep. All . . . all destroyed. I've got perhaps fifty or sixty sheets, all burnt round the edges. I've got to reconstruct what's on them. There are 60 poems of [Russell's translation of] Mandelstam, out of 220. Have you seen my poem on the funeral of Ezra?

No, I don't think I have. I've seen your poem for his eightieth birthday. You describe the funeral in your introduction to An Examination of Ezra Pound *[an anthology of essays about Pound, published in the U.S. in 1950]. How did that come about, doing that anthology?*

Well it was my idea, and I took it to various publishers. Eliot wouldn't publish it. He thought that the time was inopportune. He was very cautious.

Why did he think it was inopportune?

Well, he thought it would put the backs up of the literary establishment, who would do everything they could to keep him [Pound] inside [St. Elizabeth's Hospital in Washington]. And they did.

There were people who wanted to keep Pound inside?

All the left-wing people, you see. Which means about half.

Would Auden have been one of them?

No, Auden was very fair about Pound. Auden was a kind man, he was a good man. With all sorts of quirks and eccentricities. But he was a good chap. It was the little professors with their rigid communist prejudices. They hated him, and they hate me. . . . Where were we? Oh yes, the irony was that I then took it to a small firm of publishers with three directors of which were all Jews. And they leapt at it; they loved the book. You see, this myth of Ezra's antisemitism comes from his own stupidity, where he talked in the radio speeches about Jews: "Cromwell was a Jew! Churchill's a Jew!" Well, you know, this is like MacDiarmid shouting his head off. Ezra was playing popular demagogue, which wasn't really in him at all. He was acting it. When I first told Ezra I was going to Italy for the first time—what should I do? who should I see?—he gave me a list of four people to visit. He said nothing about them except that they're good people, "My close friends, they've done a lot to help me out over the years, I've known them for twenty or thirty years," and that sort of thing. I went to see them. They were all Jews, and very conscious of being Jews. But they loved Ezra. No problem, you see. He wasn't antisemitic—I mean, every time, every evening I went to Ezra's house there was somebody there who was Jewish, and there was no conflict about it at all.

So when Pound made those statements it was a sort of shorthand?

Yes. That is: "Jew" equaled "money-lender." I know enough about the banks to know that he was absolutely right about the harmful effects of usury and moneylending, but he was absolutely wrong to use the word "Jew." And it ruined his life. There's very little prejudice in Italy about Pound and anti-semitism. There's a book that's published in Rome—haven't got the details. I want to get it. On Ezra and usury and the banks and that sort of thing. I read it in a small magazine, published in Florence, which draws on a lot of very serious and good writers, but they're all—I won't say fascist—but they're all, you know, definitely extreme right. Not authoritarian fascism or anything like that, but the so-called traditional school, people like [Julius] Evola, who's a brilliant writer I think. But he's known as being fascist and all of that, and therefore [ignored] by the whole of the left, which means three-quarters of the literary world in Italy. You know about the big thing in Pisa University, about [Giovanni] Gentile? Gentile, as you probably know, was a brilliant philosopher. He was a marvelous educationalist. And he was Mussolini's minister of education. He founded the modern Italian school system. He also edited, off the top of his head, the whole of the first edition of the *Enciclopedia italiana*, 1928 [actually 1936], a wonderful compilation. And then, the communist resistance people murdered him, assassinated him in Florence in '43 [actually 1944]. Cowardly act. Gentile is known to have helped a great many Jews to get out of Italy or hide themselves. Recently, very late in the day, I mean fifty years late, the University of Pisa wanted to put up a *lapide* [stone] in his memory. What happened? A hundred professors objected to a *lapide* to this great man, whose only fault was having been Mussolini's minister. I wrote to the rector—naturally they haven't put the thing up—saying couldn't you solve the problem by putting up a memorial to the people who murdered him? No reply, of course [*laughs*].

. . .

There's a young man [now editing University of Salzburg Press, which published a lot of Russell's work] who is interested in the more or less avant-gardist poets, whoever they are. I just don't fit in. You see, Salzburg did three volumes of selections—selections from a five-year period. First of all there was Peter Jay with Anvil Press and my *All for the Wolves*. Then Salzburg did *More for the Wolves*, then they did *My Wild Heart*, and they accepted for publication a subsequent volume to be called *Bewildered Heart*. You see? "My wild heart," "*bewildered* heart." This "bewildered" is a play of words—there's "wild," "wilder." But this "bewildered" translates an Arabic term, which is a little bit like the Dark Night of the Soul; the mystic, who's been going along fine for a long time, just when he's just beginning to think he's seeing the truth and everything, he gets all confused and in a terrible state. Despair.

I had an amazing dream, in which I was Quintilius [a fictional silver-age Latin poet in whose persona Russell wrote a large number of comic-serious poems, including the volume *From the Apocalpyse of Quintilius*], with my queen of the Indian estate that I ruled successfully for many years, and we left the estate to our children and retired to the forest in traditional Brahman style. It was a pilgrimage that we'd been making for many years. And we thought we were doing fine; we thought we'd freed ourselves of the ego and we were living completely in the spirit. At a certain point, we come up against what is a *huge* wall—imagine a wall that is fifty meters high or a hundred meters high, with great stones mortared together. We go round and round and round, there's no gate in at all, and we just sort of lie down and weep. No way to get in. Obviously this is the wall around Paradise. Nirvana. At a certain point, a young Buddhist monk comes, and he gives us a sweet smile, and *he just walks through the wall.* It was the most wonderful dream. Later, the monk came back and helped us a great deal, and we got inside. The inside . . . I mean, I couldn't express in words how beautiful it was. Super-reality.

When did you have this dream?

Oh, about six months ago. So that's my foundation at the moment.

Have you written any poetry from that dream? You've written a lot of poetry based on dreams.

It will take a long time to come. When you get these high dreams—in fact, in my earlier life it took seven years before I could incorporate it. I hope . . . [*laughs*] I hope I get to do it before that. I don't think I'm going to live seven years. I'm not depressed about death, but the thing about death that makes me sad is that I can't go on with the work I'm doing. But of course that is a form of egoism. That's why I can't get into the Garden. You can't have it both ways. You can't have your cake and eat it. And you've got to give up one or the other. That dream was unbelievable. I could see *every* leaf, every serration on every leaf, *wonderful colors*, birds of every color and shape, singing—marvelously. Have you seen my poem "In the Woods"? Probably not. It starts off, "Bird song, self singing to self." I adore birdsong.

In a few essays, you talk about [the scholar of esoteric Islam] Henry Corbin's idea of "affective tonality." Could you describe what you mean by that?

Yes, I can't find his exact words, but it means affective tonality. I've written in quite a few essays, and also in letters to young poets who write to me, that in the very first words of a poem you have to establish a context, in time in space, out of time out of space. But you have to establish a context, but a context which has this "affective tonality"—you know the tone of the thing that's going to come. You know where you are, so to speak. Sometimes when one writes perhaps a bad poem, it's partly humorous and partly serious. That combination can be alright, as in my poem "Smoke," but it's got to be done the right way. There are no rules.

There's some place where you talk about the link between "affective tonality" and the Muses.

Yes, yes. I mean, this is inspiration. Most of the poets one meets today might have something quite interesting to say, but they don't really have any *tonality.* I wish I could find Corbin's exact words—I'll find them sometime when I reread some of his books, which I'm overdue for now.

You studied with Corbin [at the Imperial Iranian Academy of Philosophy, where Corbin taught], right?

Oh, yes, I've read almost everything by him. But they're not the sort of books you read once and put down. You have to go back to them four or five times.

Yes, they're very dense . . . The presence of Sufi ideas in your poetry—there seems to be more and more of it as time goes on.

Yes, "Albae Meditatio" [the poem discussed in the next chapter in this book] was a kind of apex of that. I don't know whether I'll ever capture that tonality again. But you see, it does open, and establish *immediately* a context and a tonality. And I think that's how it must be. You see, enormous amounts of poetry gets written today, especially in Italy, which expresses alright ideas—about getting rid of the ego and living in the spirit—but it's really only opinion, it doesn't convince you. These people are saying what they think they ought to say in order to be a poet. There's no conviction there at all.

Yes, intellect and emotion somehow are integrated in your work. I think that a lot of writers tend to do one or the other.

Yes, but very few succeed in communicating real emotion. Whereas music, modern music, is absolutely out of the world of emotion. It's not really music; it's experimentation with sound, with noise. Pop music is better than the professor's music. All theories.

[A couple of hours later, having gone to the train station to pick up Lenny Emmanuel.]

I'm writing an enormous amount, you know.

Yes, you have all these new sonnets.

I've got sixty new sonnets in the last three months. Plus two hundred, maybe three hundred lyrics, satires . . .

Have you always been drawn to writing in the sonnet form?

Oh yes, yes. I mean, when I was very young, eleven, twelve, thirteen, I read the whole of Petrarch—and *adored* it. And of course I knew the Shakespeare sonnets and the better known Elizabethan and Jacobean sonneteers. Mainly from the anthologies—the Shakespeare ones I knew very well when I was young. But I preferred the Petrarchan form. The Shakespeare sonnets are very uneven; some of them are terribly careless. I don't even think he wrote them. At any rate, from 1946 onwards I was writing sonnets quite seriously . . . Petrarch, Petrarch is the basis of the sonnet.

EMMANUEL: If you do off-rhyme, imperfect rhymes and stuff, I like that. I just don't like "Jack and Jill went up the hill to fetch a pail of water," you know.

RUSSELL: But Mother Goose is the *best* preparation for any poet, because they have every rhythm you can imagine.

FRISARDI: *Well, that's true. When I was a kid, when I got fevers, high fevers, I would get delirious often, and I would hallucinate. And the thing that would stop my hallucinations was Mother Goose rhymes.*

RUSSELL: Really? Very interesting. It makes sense to me.

FRISARDI: *I would recite them with my mother, the Mother Goose rhymes— because usually the hallucinations were pretty scary—and the Mother Goose rhymes would calm me down.*

RUSSELL: That's very interesting. I've never heard that before, but I believe it.

EMMANUEL: I've told Peter about so-called perfect rhyme, and to me, when he does his best is when he uses off-rhyme, when it doesn't take attention away from the content.

FRISARDI: *Really? Because I think sometimes, in a poem like "Theorem," there's a very exact, you know, there are strong rhymes in there.*

EMMANUEL: You like that?

FRISARDI: *I like both. I like any effect if it works, basically. And I think it can work as long as it doesn't feel forced or slow down the movement, but I don't think it has to feel forced.*

RUSSELL: When you think of a great poet of the seventeenth-century metaphysical school, like Henry Vaughn . . . Vaughn's rhymes are absolutely infantile—it's "light," "sight," "night," every time. But the things work *beautifully*. Because the rhymes tie up with the other words in the rest of the poetry. Therefore it's not just a *sound* rhyme; it's a meaning rhyme, a semantic rhyme. And I use these same words, the obvious things, very annoying in English, key words like "soul," or spirit. You can't really rhyme them. OK, you've got "hole," or "whole"—that's good: you know, "the whole soul." But the other rhymes are unusable, there are only two or three. "Dover sole" [*laughs*]—I mean, what can you do? . . .

EMMANUEL: When were you at Purdue University?

RUSSELL: It must have been in 1977.

FRISARDI: *What did you teach there?*

RUSSELL: Creative writing. I liked the black kids very much, because they used to write these stories, in their own language. The white kids would say, "But he can't even write English." I said, "But he does. He writes Black American English." That's good. It's the most living language in the United States. When I was in New York for a whole year, I used to spend every evening, or almost every evening, in the black bars on the Upper West Side. Those people, I mean, they used to be very hostile when I entered. I just politely asked for whatever I wanted. Somebody would come up to me and say, "Why're you here?" And I said, "Well, I like these places, I like your people. I'm an Englishman." "Oh, you're English, you're not American."

EMMANUEL: They liked you then?

RUSSELL: I got on marvelously with those people. So much humor, such rich language—oh, *wonderful*. Not many very good poets. What was the old man's name?

FRISARDI: *Hughes? Langston Hughes?*

RUSSELL: Langston Hughes, yes. What a dear man. I adored him. I never met Richard Wright. Interesting man, but a bit too political for me.

FRISARDI: *When did you know Langston Hughes?*

It would have been in '66. I spent late '66 and the first half of '67 entirely in New York. I had a bit of money. The Washington Square Press gave me a three-thousand-buck advance for a translation of the complete poems of Mandelstam. Of course they're all lost now; they were all burnt in that fire. For reasons of copyright, they turned down the book; they couldn't print it. Political correctness. There was no copyright. In the meantime, a gang of crooks at Texas spread the rumor around that my translations were inaccurate. Which was absolutely untrue, because the one thing I really went for was verbal accuracy. I was learning Russian at the same time I was translating Mandelstam. Lydia [Pasternak, Boris's sister] lived in Oxford, and I met her when she was reading a new batch of poems by her brother, in some organization in Bayswater, and I went along. I took a week after that absolutely ransacking the grammars of Russian. And within a week of starting Russian, I started translating Mandelstam. Obviously I had great difficulty at the beginning, because I didn't know the internal connections of words and so on. But I did some what I think quite good translations. I started out with rhyme and meter, and [a man who] was then running a review called . . . something in Montreal, I can't remember, he wrote to me—this would be 1957—"Peter, you just can't do translations into rhyme and meter. It's ridiculous." Of course the exact opposite of what I think today. Unfortunately I listened to him. And I did them into, in effect, free verse. Very natural, but without rhyme. And Russian poetry without rhyme isn't Russian poetry. Apart, from, say, Mayakovsky, who had a genius for other things. At any rate, I then translated everything that was known, everything of poetry that was known of Mandelstam. And I got to know quite a lot of Russian—of course I wasn't an expert; you'd need a five-year course to be an expert. I just did it on the side. I was a busy book seller. Ten hours a day in the shop, a few hours a day with my family, my young son, my wife then, digging the garden, coping with all the domestic problems. You know how it is. Then when I came to Italy, I did a great many more. And as I say, Washington Square Press gave me this big advance, three thousand dollars—Robert Paine was at the back of it. I haven't heard from Robert for about twenty years; I presume he's just died. He looked like he was going to die when I last saw him. Dear, sweet man. I think he had a terrible pasty face, and a *tremore*, you know. And I thought, well, dear Robert, you're not going to last long. Then, as I say, they never published the book, they never sent my manuscript back. Of course, I had copies. Because these people at Texas university wanted their own translations to go in. And in the end, you know, Penguin Books took up . . . William . . . what's his name? William . . . An American poet. A very well known poet, very good poet too. He's done a lot of translations from Spanish. I think he does know Spanish, but he certainly don't know Russian. He, with the help of a prof at Princeton did an edition of Mandelstam for Penguin, which is, you might say, the standard Mandelstam today.

Was it Merwin?

Merwin, yes. W. S. Merwin. Now I met W. S. Merwin when he was just starting. Must have been '53, '54. Very nice man, you know. I liked him very much. But we've lost contact. He hasn't answered letters, which is not very nice. But he's a good poet.

You said on the phone last night that you didn't really like [Eugenio] Montale, that you thought Montale was just too pessimistic. But I think that a book like La bufera [The Storm] *is not just pessimistic.*

You think it's OK? I find, even his earlier work, which everybody says is better than his later work, I find it sort of hopelessly negative. I mean, OK, he had a wonderful sense of the balance of consonants and vowels, syllables, and meter, and so on. It is free verse but it's free verse which is really strict. It's almost Parnassian. But it's so totally negative. Nothing works in his world. And he was like that as a person—he never had a good word to say for *anybody*, unless it was to his advantage to write it in the [Milan newspaper] *Corriere della Sera*. Montale was a great disappointment to me. I read Montale first when I came to Italy in '47, and I was impressed by his tremendous control of rhythm. And I wasn't that much put off by the pessimism at that phase. A young fellow—I was, what? twenty-six, twenty-seven—is easily duped by a big reputation. I thought, "Well, I *ought* to like Montale, so I *will* like Montale." Not entirely honest. Rereading him recently . . .

Which one? His first book?

I've read everything up to the end of *La bufera*. I've got to read *Satura* and the late ones.

So you thought La bufera *is also very negative?*

Terribly negative.

Because I thought that with the two muse figures, Clizia and La Volpe, there's a beautiful remaking of the dolce stil novo *[Dante's and other Tuscan poets' "sweet new style"] conceits.*

Really? Maybe you're right. Maybe it was just my mood in Sicily this summer.

What did Pound think of Montale?

He never mentioned Montale. Montale never spoke to Pound. I remember, about a year before Pound's death, they were on the same platform, at the Fondazione Cini; it's the most important platform in Venezia. They didn't speak to each other. Montale—being the great antifascist—wouldn't speak to the old man. Disgusting; absolutely disgusting. Because Pound was very open to everybody—left, right, center. . . . There is this brilliant lady from the University of Genoa who has written two very long, extremely brilliant essays on my sonnets. What is very interesting is she points out that Peter Russell is known as the student of Pound and has totally rejected Pound's views on the sonnet.

I remember reading somewhere that you found in Petrarch the complex syntax and rhetoric that Pound didn't like.

You see, Pound, who had a marvelous sense of all literature, was still a child of his own time—the prewar period. He was formed between, say, 1902 and 1912. And he wanted to be with the times, he wanted to be an *avant-gardiste.*

He was reacting against the excesses of Victorian poetry.

Oh, absolutely! He was right, he was right. I mean, you take Pound on Milton. Pound dismissed Milton. Eliot, following him, dismisses Milton.

And Shelley. They hated Shelley.

Yes, they were children of their time—in a bad sense. Eliot and Pound had certain good reasons to warn us against Miltonianism. Now, we need somebody to encourage people to write like Milton. Both of them will be right.

That is, in 1912, it was wise to advise young poets to avoid writing like Milton. Now, I think, we need to advise young poets to write *like* Milton.

[Various random comments. Then Russell talks about a poem he's working on, his process of working on it.]

I'm never in a hurry to write a poem. I start off maybe with only two words. You take that idea of "fickle imagination"—where am I going to go from there? Am I going to be in favor of imagination or against imagination? Of course, I'm going to be both. I'm in no hurry. I'm going to read some more Góngora, some more Ernst Jünger. . . . You've got to look up Ernst Jünger.

EMMANUEL: What did he say?

RUSSELL: Well, he was a man who traveled around, virtually everywhere. He'd stay in a particular place for six months, a year. He seemed to know every leaf of every plant, every insect, every bird, everything, all the different types of people, the bartenders, and the local people. He really got himself *right* into life, and he wrote perhaps a hundred books. I'm reading them all in Italian, because I don't know who publishes them in English. I can read them in German but it slows me down, you know. I read German about one-fifth the speed that I can read Italian, one-tenth of the speed that I read English. But then the translations have got to be good. And there's this article by him—I forget which collection it's in but it's in one of his major books—on the relations and the nature of consonants and vowels. He takes off from Jacob Grimm. Grimm, of course, is the great source of all our knowledge of language. If you want to know about language, you've got to read the five huge volumes of Jacob Grimm. His brother Wilhelm also wrote really wonderful things, but Jacob, I think, was really the seminal man. Like the two Schlegel brothers. You know, you have to read all of Schlegel, two of them. Those German romantics were just *fantastic*. Novalis, I think, I mean, Novalis died at twenty-five years old. The *profundity* of that young man. I mean, Keats fades into nothing beside Novalis.

I read all these great German romantics when I was a kid at school. When I was studying biology and chemistry as a kid at school, high school, it was absolutely necessary to learn German, to read the best texts on those subjects. I went out to Germany in '39, June till September '39. I stayed with a wonderful family, a dear old professor of history at the University of

Heidelberg. Poor old chap, not being a member of the Nazi Party, was finding it very difficult to be accepted. He had three young children growing up, who were all passionate Nazis, and he took paying guests. Well, I found this man through some agency in London, and I went out and stayed with him at some ludicrously small amount per month. And the old boy took to me, he took me around, he was *in*defatigable. He walked me round all Heidelberg, up the Neckar River. And, to all the . . . you know, the festival of course with plays by all the great German dramatists—Goethe, Schiller. He taught me *so much*, and he introduced me to the German lyric poets. I read Goethe, Hölderlin, Novalis, all of them. Marvelous. I had with me the *Oxford Book of German Verse*, which was not bad, it was a good selection, but of course he introduced me to a lot more.

. . .

FRISARDI: *Peter, in your lectures* Dante and Islam *you say how Dante, even though he learned so much from Islam, kept a provincial attitude toward it, and had a kind of bigotry toward Islam which was characteristic of the time. But why did he do that, when he took so much and he learned so much from these great [Muslim] writers?*

Well, I think he was of his own time. If I cast out whoever our enemies are now, we reject everything that they have. And he was the same. He put Muhammad in hell, Ali in hell.

He puts them with the schismatics.

Yes. And we haven't gotten beyond them in our own time, six hundred years after Dante. What can you do? Dante wasn't perfect; he was a child of his own time. And there's no doubt whatever Dante had known very many people who knew the Middle East and the Arab world, the Persian world, extremely well. Templars and other people who would come back after thirty years of living there, after they'd married Arab wives or Persian wives. In that age, when there weren't manuscripts and printed books of everything, people recited hundreds of lines from, let's say, the Arab or Persian poets, translated into Italian. I don't say Dante knew Arab, because I don't believe so. But he must have known many Arabs or Persians who recited these things for him in Italian or Latin, and of course being the great genius that he was he picked up the whole idea. He probably never heard of Ibn ʿArabī, but he knew the whole of Ibn ʿArabī.

I wonder why, in the modern West, there is there such a resistance to ecstatic spiritual poetry, unlike, say, in earlier times? The ecstatic spirituality that comes through Dante and the dolce stil novo *poets, or the Sufi poets.*

You see, I would put it this way. Until the beginnings of the so-called Renaissance, there was no real difference between Orient and Occident. From the beginnings of the Renaissance, the myth of the "mysterious Orient" begins: the Oriental whose mind you can't understand. Absolute nonsense. Indians, *Mussulmani* [Muslims], Buddhists, Taoists—absolutely rational sensible people, that we can understand if we *want* to. I was there as a young man. I spent time in India, Malaya, with the Chinese of course—the Chinese are dominant in Malaya—Thailand, the south of China, and had many many contacts with the Japanese. At the end of the war we had about twenty Japanese officers, who were our prisoners, and I'd say we treated them very well. *Officially* we had to keep them segregated. In fact, of course, we chatted with them. Most of them spoke very good Burmese. I didn't understand Japanese, but because they'd been there in Burma for three years, they spoke quite good Burmese, and I spoke absolutely fluent Burmese. We could communicate. And they introduced me to all the major Japanese ideas. . . . And I got all sorts of ideas out of them. Wonderful things.

. . .

I believe that our society is a spiritual wasteland and that the arts can do something about that.

It's the big problem of today. Essential. You see, each of us, we have to do our own little thing towards this big objective. Each individual has to do some small thing towards it. When it's all added up, the serious individuals will have contributed an enormous amount to a higher view of what we humans need.

Emmanuel: Peter, what's the small thing that you think you have to act against? The materialism?

RUSSELL: Well, materialism, but there's *indifferentismo*. You see, most people are quite content to pass their lives being amused by television: birth, television, death. Then there's a higher life, which is based on what we vaguely call the soul. The soul is full of completely contradictory things. All the different emotions, and ideas, and reasons. And then there's the spirit, which is completely free from the ego or *io* ["I"]. It's really the mind of God, the Divine Mind.

FRISARDI: *What kind of change would be most needed for a renaissance in poetry and culture?*

A new poetry has got to come absolutely spontaneously. No theory. It's no good reading the fucking—excellent—*Enciclopedia di Princeton [points to* The Princeton Encyclopedia of Poetry and Poetics, *on shelf next to table]*. It's got to come from the heart, from the balls, from the toes—from every part of our body. I have no program for the future of poetry, because I believe it will come out of a new . . . a new . . . I'm trying to find a good word. A new attitude.

An awakening.

Yeah, an awakening. A renaissance. But, you see, a renaissance is not going to be an academic program, which says, "The old renaissance was like this, the new renaissance is going to be like this." It's just going to come out of absolute spontaneity. It may come out of some housewife—who knows? from West Lafayette, the worst place ever—who has a wonderful vision of the possibilities and writes it.

Peter Russell's "Albae Meditatio"

✳

"A LBAE Meditatio" was one of its Peter Russell's own favorite poems among his works, as he told me soon after I got to know him in spring 2000, and I agree that it is a high point of his poetry. The poem is dated September 1st, 1991; it was first published as the final poem of five in a self-published chapbook, *The Progress of the Soul*.[1]

In an issue of his literary journal *Nine* in the late 1940s, Russell described the artist's task as "continuing the dance of the ages," and in fact his rich and imaginative engagement with many of the world's cultures and languages past and present comes through in all his writing. At the same time, Russell emphasized that it matters how we approach cultural heritage. He liked to quote Pound in this regard: "Tradition inheres in the images of the gods and gets lost in dogmatic definitions"; and he once described Pound in words that apply equally to Russell himself: "A gregarious man and very permeable to ideas of a heterogeneous nature, he could hardly help becoming *simultaneously* a traditionalist and an avant-gardist."[2] Indeed, Russell in the span of his work is protean and multifaceted. The poet Richard Berengarten has outlined Russell's main poetic identities: traditional lyricist, experimental post-Poundian modernist, and comic poet of

---

1. For copyright reasons, I have not quoted extensively from "Albae Meditatio." Interested readers can find it in Russell's late collection *My Wild Heart*, as well as in an Italian selected poems, *Poesie dal Valdarno*. The latter prints the poem in its final version, very slightly changed from the earlier version (the line "I am she," discussed near the end of this essay, was added).

2. Russell, *Something About Poetry*, 141.

Rabelaisian appetites and vitriol. I would add to this list visionary elegist—and this is where "Albae Meditatio" fits into his overall work.

From at least the 1950s on, Russell wrote a number of long poems which draw on his wide erudition and life experience, typically in metrically variable lines or free verse that give the poet space to follow the thread of his thought and imagination. A collection of Russell's published in 1981, *Elemental Discourses*, consists of forty or so such poems, which Russell's introduction to that book calls "Contemplations." He writes that he intended his poems in this mode to be "sacred spaces cut out of the chaos of the profane consciousness, spaces in which to consider and observe, to concentrate the mind and to come nearer to an understanding of the realities of existence." A "sacred space cut out" is the basic meaning of *temenos*, from *temnein*, "to cut," as Russell also states in this passage. He goes on to say that in his poetic "Contemplations" there is a constant shift of focus "between the corporeal, the soul or psychic; and the noetic, or intuitive fields."[3] As we find in "Albae Meditatio," this sort of composition in Russell's work is "a process in which the consciousness starts out from one of these three levels but may focus on 'subject-matter' either of the same or of a different level."[4] Their author is committed simultaneously to embodied, sensuous experience and to seeking openings into the underlying intuitive and interior dimension of things. All the poems of *Elemental Discourses* are shaped by the author's considerable conceptual ambition. Because thought plays such an active role in these visionary elegies, they are never passive stream-of-consciousness registers of sensations. Russell often chided "imagist" poetry for being only sensuous and exterior, lacking in intellect and therefore ultimately an expression of modernist spiritual passivity. What I very much enjoy about Russell's "Contemplations" is their uncompromising hermetic-philosophical searchingness, the breadth of their subject matter, their holistic embrace of life, and their joie de vivre and spirit of curiosity and quest. They are a refreshing contrast to the self-imposed narrowness and cultural provincialism of much contemporary poetry.

However, while Russell strives in these pieces for connections and associations, images, literary allusions, thoughts, and sounds that will integrate the disconnected fragments of contemporary experience, they tend to be lacking in finish and cohesiveness. They always have something interesting and worthwhile to say, but the mix of naturalistic observation, intuitive

3. Russell, *Elemental Discourses*, 45.
4. Russell, *Elemental Discourses*, 45.

insight, and erudition often doesn't fully gel and therefore one poem tends to blend into another, fading in the reader's memory soon after the book is closed. "Albae Meditatio" represents Russell's hard-earned mastery of what he had been striving for in his earlier pieces on this genre. In the later poem these various elements, including book learning, harmonize into a sustained ecstatic hymn.[5]

The opening lines from one of his "Contemplations" from the 1960s, included in *Elemental Discourses*, will illustrate Russell's earlier explorations in this mode:

> Life is a celebration not a search for success.
> In the grey street to see visions of violet roses
> And snow-buntings crowding in the black grass of the gutter;
> A solitary heron with an eel in its beak
> Circling the Stock Exchange. It is life, not death,
> Celebration, not success, we must offer
> To our wives, our children, our mistresses . . . ("A Celebration")

The theme of exuberant participation in life is a constant in Russell's writing; and the attention to natural detail is also characteristic. Unfortunately, the pontificating tone in the final lines of this excerpt weighs down the symbolic possibilities that are just starting to take flight. The opening imagery, and notably the birds (in his youth Russell wrote a sonnet for every bird on the British Bird List—four hundred of them), are echoed in "Albae Meditatio." In "A Celebration" the opening scene-setting is followed up by the sort of intuitive meandering between thought, symbol, learned allusion, and personal utterance that we find in "Albae Meditatio." The later poem, however, is a major step forward from, or a consolidation of, earlier compositions such as this. Now, in seven lines of great self-assurance, we move not only between images but between levels of reality:

> Already it's getting light and the first birds
> Are twittering in the walnut tree, and you
> Are hidden everywhere from my fallacious eye.
> Some of the pale green leaves at this hour
> Appear bright yellow, smooth grey of the walnut bark
> Jet like the young girl's cable braids swinging like bell ropes.
>
> There is a mirror you cannot see and a rose in it.

5. Russell's other most realized poem in this genre, though its style is quite different (more Poundian-elliptical) than that of "Albae Meditatio," is *Paysages Legendaires*, published by Enitharmon Press in 1971. Used copies of this book can be found online, and a quick search did turn up a copy of *Elemental Discourses* as well.

The texture of this passage, which Russell maintains through all twelve verse paragraphs and 137 lines of "Albae Meditatio," creates *Stimmung*, as he liked to call it, atmosphere; or, as he would refer to it in the interview in the previous chapter, "affective tonality" (a term he took from the great scholar of esoteric Islam Henry Corbin). To quote Russell:

> I've written in quite a few essays, and also in letters to young poets who write to me, that in the very first words of a poem you have to establish a context, in time in space, out of time out of space. But you have to establish a context, a context which has this "affective tonality." You know the tone of the thing that's going to come. You know where you are, so to speak.

When I mentioned to him that I recalled from one of his essays that he associated affective tonality with the Muses, Russell responded: "Yes, yes. I mean, this is inspiration. Most of the poets one meets today might have something quite interesting to say, but they don't really have any *tonality*." In writing about the visionary recitals of Avicenna and Suhrawardī, Corbin emphasizes the *personhood* of the encounters, the intimacy that made the active intelligence appear to these sages as angelic *presences*—this is the context in which Corbin uses the word *tonality*. Russell was right that "Albae Meditatio" is permeated by this elusive quality; it is not merely *about* its subject, as the earlier "Contemplations" often had been (although they too had stretches of true and lucid beauty), but to read it is to *participate* in the intuition that went into its making. Also notable is the broad erudition in the poem—erudition which would not matter at all, especially in a poem, except for the fact that it is so well assimilated into the flow of the poetry. "Albae Meditatio" is an echo chamber of Russell's vast and intimate knowledge of literary traditions, including the western love lyric, the King James Bible, the Persian ghazal, and modernist *vers libre*. The long lines gather momentum in clusters, alternating between declarative simplicity and scriptural or prophetic, elevated tone.

The poem opens with an indirect question: how is it possible to penetrate beneath the surface of the dazzling beauty of the world if "you" (the elusive Presence or being of things) "Are hidden everywhere from my fallacious eye"? The second verse paragraph expands on this thought. Given "Green leaves, running water, a beautiful face," how can we "love these things with a passion pure but intense?" that is, with an aesthetic response that does not blind us to the metaphysical transparency of things. We may be aware that beneath or behind the world of appearances, "There is a mirror you cannot see and a rose in it"—the mirror, that is, of archetypal forms—but it is difficult, to say the least, to gain access to this mirror of nature, since something is "between my eye and the passing of Beauty." No matter how we may try to overcome the limitation, perception is subjective, conditioned by "The prism of air" and the bending "in perpetual duel [of] the living rods." In a lovely intuitive move, Russell converts the rods, the cells of the retina, into lances squaring off for a joust. As we shall see, this is just one of the many oppositions that appear in the poem. The reference in this verse paragraph to "The young boy with his cap awry" draws on Sufi poetic tradition, which in turn is based on a hadith in which the Prophet declares, "I saw my Lord in the shape of a beautiful young man, with his cap awry." To the chagrin of more orthodox Muslims, the Persian poets used the phrase *kaj-kulah*, "with his cap awry," in poetic descriptions of the human beloved as a manifestation of divine beauty, as distant from the lover as God himself.

Given this wish to stay true to immediate sensuous experience in the fullness of desire, while not abandoning contemplative intellect to the Heraclitean flux, it is not hard to understand why Russell would be drawn to theologies of the Platonic ascent to the One through the path of beauty ("Beauty is a ladder / To higher branches"), and especially to the various expressions of theophanic beauty among the poets of the Sufi tradition. As this poem states several times, love may be an "illusion" from the point of view of reason, but it "is its own reality," like metaphor or symbol, which is "a bridge to reality" that carries a suprarational truth. One of Russell's favorite quotations in this regard was from the German romantic poet Novalis, who wrote that illusions are essential to truth; as well as Yeats's statement near the end of his life that though we cannot know the truth, we may embody it. The second verse paragraph concludes with the poet staking claim to his position in relation to the intelligible world and the world of the senses: he accepts that he dwells in the space between them, content with Proclus's so-called "second life of the soul." The poet is not an ascetic seeking out contemplation of the One in the "first life of the soul," or imageless intellectual contemplation; rather he is "willing to be tossed to and fro on the wind / Of whatever makes for cohesion in our mutable world." As the poem states in a particularly beautiful image, this poet is content to be a "straw to Love's amber."

In his introduction to his collection *Venice Poems* 1965 (1995), Russell refers to the Neoplatonist Proclus's commentary on Plato's *Republic*, which outlines the "three lives of the soul." The first, or mystic life, consists of the desire of the highest part of the soul to be with the One—Plotinus's "flight of the alone to the Alone." The second expresses an intelligible essence in images, much as in Corbin's *mundus imaginalis*, or imaginal world; that is, it uses symbols, metaphors, figures of speech in the enactment of a vision-ary recital in a middle realm between pure spirit and formless matter. And lastly, quoting Proclus, Russell writes that the third life of the soul "accords with its inferior powers, and energizes with them, employing phantasies and irrational senses, being entirely filled with things of a subordinate nature."[6] As Russell concludes, with regard to the third life of the soul: "I can't think of a better description of most recent poetry than this." These distinctions are important in Russell's poetic vision and practice, and in particular in "Albae Meditatio," since the Platonic "mania" of poetic inspiration is some-thing quite different from the mania or madness of the third life of the soul. In "Albae Meditatio," as in Platonic and later tradition, the poetic fury is closely allied with erotic frenzy or inspiration, but with an eye toward the truth of beauty rather than self-referential and delusional "phantasies." As Yeats was fond of quoting from the *Chaldean Oracles*: "Stoop not down to the darkly splendid world wherein continually lies a faithless depth and Hades wrapped in cloud, delighting in unintelligible images." *Furor divinus* in the proper sense is associated with the penetration of that darkness by the light of poetic intuition, to which the rich learning that lines the veins of "Albae Meditatio" is dedicated.

An essay by Parvin Loloi published in a *Swansea Review* special issue dedicated to Russell (2000) explicates the dense Sufi background to "Albae Meditatio." I have already drawn on some of Loloi's insights in my observa-tions above. Although I eventually became familiar with Sufi ideas, unlike when I first encountered this poem, Russell's poem communicates its sym-bolic and poetic content compellingly even to a reader without erudition in this area. This to me is one of the surest indications of the poem's success; I was fully drawn into its world even before I could articulate or explain some of its key allusions. In any case, the world of western ecstatic love poetry and its esoteric ramifications has long been quite familiar to me through Dante and his poet-friends, and this too permeates Russell's poem. As Loloi says, the notion that the phenomenal world is a manifestation of divine beauty with which the aspirant seeks to be united is a central tenet of Sufi teaching, yet it is also to be found in other sources—St. Bonaventure,

---

6. Russell, *Venice Poems*, 14.

for instance, or the Italian *dolce stil novo* poets. But there is no doubt that the Sufi background predominates in Russell's poem.

Loloi explains that "Albae Meditatio" is modeled largely on *Naẓm al-Sulūk*, or *The Poem of the Way* (also known as the *Tā'iyyat al-Kubrā*, or *The Great Poem in the Letter "T"*), by one of the greatest Sufi poets, the Egyptian Ibn al-Fāriḍ (1181–1235). Al-Fāriḍ, as Russell says in his long essay "The Figure of Woman in Islamic and Christian Love Poetry of the Middle Ages,"[7] was a main source of the standard tropes and dramatis personae of love familiar to us from the troubadours, the *Romance of the Rose*, and the courtly love poets. Loloi writes that the *Tā'iyyat* is a meditation on divine love and the mystic's progress on the way of love toward eventual union with the Beloved—and this certainly does describe the content of "Albae Meditatio." Also central to this background—and again the Sufi tradition and some western cognate traditions are nearly indistinguishable in this regard—is that the divine is approached in its feminine form: woman is the mirror in which the male seeker contemplates the image of his very Self. As Russell quotes the Jungian Erich Neumann in his essay, "the feminine-maternal wisdom is no abstract, disinterested knowledge, but a wisdom of loving participation."[8] The image of the Creative Feminine is the means by which the mystic or poet can apprehend God in the aspect of creative divinity, as Sophia, Shekinah, or the Virgin Mother—the image of Sapientia in the books of Solomon being a particularly influential instance of this. In the ecstatic poetic tradition that Russell follows, then, the Creator is feminine and the aspiration for union with the living Word is portrayed in terms of a longing for union with the Beloved. Love in all its forms is ultimately this longing for self-transcendent union, wherein, as Ḥāfiẓ famously puts it, the moth is destined to burn in the flame.

Loloi's essay is an invaluable aid for penetrating deeper into the rich symbolism of "Albae Meditatio." For example, the image of the poet as "a straw to Love's amber" draws on the observation, going back as far as Thales, of amber's electrostatic properties. Thales noticed that by rubbing a piece of amber on fur, small bits of straw or feather were attracted to it, and like other ancients after him he mistakenly identified this effect as magnetism rather than static electricity. The Sufi poets picked up on the tradition from antiquity. As Loloi writes: "The traditional magnetic properties of amber were said to attract even the smallest piece of straw. In fact in Persian,

---

7. Russell, "Figure of Woman," in *Image of Woman*, 33–97.
8. Russell, "Figure of Woman," in *Image of Woman*, 42.

the word for straw is *Kah*, and amber is called *Kahrubba*, which literally means 'the straw-robber.' Persian poets often compare themselves to small pieces of straw which are attracted to amber like the lover to the Beloved."[9] The metaphor is particularly apt when we recall the color of amber, whose translucence glows like dark honey when held in the light. To be drawn to it, then, against one's will as it were, has to do with being fatally attracted to something that is both bodily and spiritual, suffused by light that is given an earthy tone by the attachments of human love.

The poem continues in the third verse paragraph with further exploration of the themes already introduced. Love in the fullest sense breaks self-will, so that

> . . . there are people who think that Love is a mere illusion,
> Like physicians and vendors of money and weapons
> And the learned in universities and the assessors of culture,

but also the religiously dogmatic or self-righteous and Pharisees of all stripes—in contrast to the Dionysian and primitive-Christian imagery where "Stone . . . is bread, is living flesh," and where "the rough wine of the country is Love himself." Love, whether erotic or spiritual or both at once, is self-surrender. Sufi use of the symbolism of wine is well known, including its heterodox implications in the context of abstemious Islam; and Christian poets such as Dante, as well as the Bible itself, also draw on the imagery of intoxication to communicate the sense of ecstatic spiritual experience. Russell quotes Ibn al-Fāriḍ's ode on wine, the *Khamrīyah*: "In memory of the Beloved we quaffed a vintage that made us drunk before the creation of the vine."[10] In addition, as Russell puts it in his poem and as the tradition of love poetry both East and West has stated countless times, "There is no sweeter poison to drink than Love"—love is both sickness and its own cure. It flays the lover of his thick skin, "the cat o'nine tails that strips off the skin," which is probably an allusion to Marsyas, who, having lost his musical challenge to Apollo, was flayed by the god—the fate of any poet who experiences inspiration. The heat of love burns away the dross of the ego, "A ferocious burnishing that leaves only light to the eye"—and also leaves behind "a coat of many colours."

This latter phrase quotes the King James translation of Genesis 37:3, where Jacob endows his favorite son, Joseph, with such a garment. Russell

---

9. Loloi, "Sufi Elements," 64.

10. Russell, "Figure of Woman," in *Image of Woman*, 62.

also alludes here to the Gnostic *Hymn of the Pearl*, from the apocryphal *Acts of Thomas*. In this story a boy who is the son of "the king of kings" is sent to Egypt to recover a pearl from a serpent. While he is in Egypt—a symbol of the blindness of the gross material state—he forgets his origin. When a letter from the king reminds him of his mission, he regains the pearl and brings it home—whereupon he is emblazoned with a radiant many-colored robe. The "pearl of great price" is a well-known symbol from the Gospels; and as Loloi says, for the Sufis the pearl in the oyster symbolizes the wisdom within the moist cavity of the heart. The oyster-pearl, as well as the rose mentioned earlier, are both evocative of the female sexual organs and of feminine inwardness and depth. "Albae Meditatio" itself could be taken to mean "Meditation of the White Pearl," even as it alludes to dawn, *alba*, in the Provençal and later poetic genre of the aubade (a name that derives from *albus*, or "white"), in which lovers enjoy the sweetness of being together at dawn even as they know they must separate soon.

In the next two verse paragraphs, the feminine imagery takes on an actual voice, the phantom cry from the water's depth, "a woman's cry" that is "the cry of Love himself." A key line of the poem tells us here that "Her very veils are Revelation itself"—a return to the poem's opening imagery of outward beauty pregnant with meaning that appears inaccessible to the sense-bound mind but which fills the receptive viewer with the *feeling* or anticipation of epiphany. Russell sets apart these two stanzas as a pair of tercets, drawing attention to the connections between them and to their pivotal place in the poem. The reference here to "Her black tresses" which "conceal the mole in her white neck, / But . . . display oceans of shining darkness," will be familiar to even a casual anglophone reader of Sufi poetry. Sufi poets like Shabistarī in his *Garden of Mystery* combine the allure of the beautiful, shiny dark hair of the beloved with contemplative profundity. The hair of a lover in the heightened state of love can feel like the quintessence of creation's mystery. "Oceans of shining darkness" gives a sense of this unfathomable depth. Certainly in Dante and other visionary poets the ocean is a common symbol for God, to whom the soul seeks always to return like a stream or a drop of water. Loloi explains that "the mole in her white neck" in Persian Sufi poetry denotes unity, and because it is black it resembles the divine presence which is hidden or invisible to ordinary perception. As we have seen, Russell's poem oscillates between exalted feeling and the pang of being unable to apprehend the essential reality within the appearances of things. And yet, this very veil is "Revelation itself." The Mystery is actually the least hidden thing, if only we open our eyes to it.

The next verse paragraph expands on the notion that the veil is Revelation: the image of the Woman's face appears in a black pool, in which a rose is visible: "A vision of clouds and roses, the clouds themselves are roses, / The roses themselves are light, the light is clouds." Note the union of opposites, since the clouds have to do with evanescence and motion, even as they can be rose-like in appearance. And for a further paradox, even the Empyrean, the tenth celestial sphere which in Dante's cosmology is the absolute stillness of God, "is intense motion, utterly at rest."

In the next verse paragraph the antinomian and heterodox themes that occur throughout the poem appear in an allusion to the story of Sheikh Ṣanʿān, told in ʿAṭṭār's great parable *The Conference of the Birds* (*Manṭiq al-ṭayr*). In this story a pious Sheikh falls in love with a Christian girl and subsequently takes to herding her swine. With this action—of course, the eating of pig flesh is forbidden in Islam, so rote orthodoxy is challenged here—the Sheikh has opted for the spirit over the letter of the Law, since "Without desire, neither a man nor the nightingale can sing"; and so, "The Sheikh has broken his pens in bewilderment, / The pious girl has given succour to an Infidel." In my interview with him, Russell explained a title he was planning for a poetry collection (which, it turned out, would never come to light), *My Bewildered Heart*: "This 'bewildered' is a play of words— there's 'wild,' 'wilder.' But this 'bewildered' translates an Arabic term [ḥayra], which is a little bit like the Dark Night of the Soul; the mystic, who's been going along fine for a long time, just when he's just beginning to think he's seeing the truth and everything, he gets all confused and in a terrible state. Despair." And as Russell writes in "The Figure of Woman," the frequent trope in Sufi poetry of the nightingale yearning for the rose represents the soul's longing for eternal Beauty; and "Longing is the highest state the soul can reach, for it results in creativity, whereas union brings about silence and annihilation."[11] Wisdom itself, in the person of the Sheikh, is confounded by this desire, like Blake's representations of Job, whose conventional religiosity is gutted and deepened, forced to let go of self-satisfied piety, when he is put to the test. Similarly, the Sheikh has to let go of his preconceptions and his previous proscriptions, all for the love of a Christian girl; and the pious girl likewise has broken the rules by giving "succour to an Infidel."

11. Russell, "Figure of Woman," in *Image of Woman*, 55.

In the following verse paragraph we are brought back to the scene of dawn, where "The air is an oil of roses distilled in the dew"—an air that "burns with a light blue flame, silent as moonlight," in which all the vivid sensations and experiences of the active waking life exist in the timeless present. "Goldsmiths' hammering in the bazaar" recalls Yeats's Byzantium; and there are also the voices of children playing in the square ("though," as Russell says in the next stanza, "the City is three hundred miles out of earshot"), and at the same time the poet is witness to the "silence of deserts." Since the boundary now is blurred between self and other, subject and object, consciousness is acentric and omnipresent. Both "The voices of spaces, and the spaces between the voices" in the play of appearances are phantom-like: real and unreal, substantial and fleeting. Activity and rest ultimately are both forms of "the yearning of all creatures for home," and the elusive yet essential factor of all manifestation is "Spirit . . . that never knew body." In "Albae Meditatio," the voices of past, present, and future are folded within the veil of nature, where "The states of mind of the gnostic seek out and find / These thousands of tongues, unforgetting, and thousands more."

The next verse paragraph opens with a clear allusion to the Song of Songs ("I shall pursue the woman to the new pastures where rain has fallen"), though the pastoral imagery associated with erotic love is found in other contexts as well. Now the contrasting elements of activity and rest, sensuousness and intellect, orthodoxy and heterodoxy, culminate in the sounds of life within the silence referred to in the previous stanza; all are resolved in the lovely simplicity of the following, psalm-like lines: "It is the silence of these sounds that knits my mind, / And the roar of many waters in the night refreshes me." Images of the conjunction of opposites culminate in the tension between the rod of Mosaic law, used to slay "the Pharaoh of worldly existence," and the magical wand of Hesiod, which the Muses bestowed on the shepherd-poet and with which he "harmonized worlds," initiating the great poetic tradition of the West. The oppositions are reconciled in the love that burns through them like sun through fog; this is the insight brought into the poem at this point by Somnun the Lover, a tenth-century Sufi saint who was called "the Lover" because of his poems and discourses on mystical love. Somnun's story is told in 'Aṭṭār's *Tazkirat al-Awliyā* (*Muslim Saints and Mystics*, in A. J. Arberry's translation of selections from it). Unlike many of the Sufi masters, Somnun emphasized voluntarist love over sapiential gnosis. As Russell writes in the lines following the mention of Somnun: "you cannot define anything / Unless in terms more subtle than that thing. / There is nothing subtler than Love." This forms a syllogistic argument that forces the conclusion: Love is the fundamental term for all definitions, and as such it cannot be defined. Thus it escapes the notice of a Kant or a Hegel, who think it outside their consideration. The poet, rather, surrenders to it, throwing in his lot with the "Muses, envious of the love-crazed mystics," and in an image harkening back to that of the straw drawn to amber, content to be like a fruit fly, Drosophila, caught in the web of the harvester, Death.

A question arises here: why does Russell choose a scientific name, "Drosophila," rather than the common expression, "fruit fly"? An aspect of Russell's voracious curiosity certainly was etymology and wordplay; and he was an avid reader of scientific studies as well. The word *Drosophila* comes from the Greek *drosos*, dew or water, and *phila*, love: the fruit fly as a lover of moisture or dew. It would seem, then, that Russell's word choice here is an extension of the water imagery we have noted earlier in the poem, as well as with its association with the feminine archetype—to the feminine (or "harvester") as the bringer of death to the lover-aspirant's ego. As Russell writes about Dante and Beatrice, where Beatrice is Dante's initiator into the mystery of death:

> Wisdom on earth, for the individual seeker or Lover . . . appears as the earthly figure of Beatrice. She is, you might say, cut down to the measure of the limits of individual possible intellect. When that is transcended, that earthly wisdom dies away and returns to Heaven and the Angels as the Heavenly Wisdom or *nous*, *ruah* or active intellect, the domain of pure contemplation or the Empyrean.[12]

This brings us to a guiding theme of "Albae Meditatio": the so-called *fanā*, or death to the self, of mystical Islam; parallel to what was known in medieval Christianity as the *excessus mentis*, or leaving behind of the ego-conditioned mind. The lines I have referred to about "Rapture" calling out "in rut for cleaving rupture," writes Loloi, are drawn directly from Ibn al-Fāriḍ, who says: "Thus (in my experience) the 'below-ness' of earth is the 'above-ness' of the aether, because of the closing of that which I cleave asunder: and the cleavage of that which was closed is only the outward aspect of my way." As R. A. Nicholson comments on this passage in al-Fāriḍ:

> The phrase, "because of the closing, etc." is borrowed from Kor. 21,31: "Did not the unbelievers discern that the heavens and the

---

12. Russell, "Figure of Woman," in *Image of Woman*, 86.

earth were closed until We clave them asunder and made every living thing of the water (that gushed forth)? . . . Ibn 'l-Farid evidently signifies by "the closing" that state which he elsewhere calls "union" (*jam'*), *i.e.* Being viewed synthetically as the inner unity in which all distinctions are reconciled, and by "the cleavage of that which was closed" the state of "separation" (*tafriqa*), *i.e.* Being viewed analytically in its external and phenomenal aspect.[13]

As Loloi explains, the three kinds or stages of *fanā'* structure the progression of "Albae Meditatio." Russell himself writes about these three stages, again in the essay mentioned earlier, citing Akbarābādi's commentary on Rūmī. In the first *fanā'* (dissolution), the essence of the creature disappears and is extinguished in the essence of God, like a drop of water in the ocean—and we have already referred to the ocean imagery earlier in the poem, in the context of the shining black hair of the beloved. The stripping off of the lover's outer skin and the appearance of the coat of many colors are also images for this phase. In the second *fanā'* (annihilation), the attributes of the creature extinguish themselves in the attributes of God, the human attributes being substituted by divine ones; God becomes the ears and eyes of the devotee. This stage is introduced in "Albae Meditatio" by the Sheikh's bewilderment when "The pious girl has given succour to an Infidel"; after which "The air is an oil of roses" and the individual consciousness of the poet is replaced by the omnipresent awareness of the "Spirit . . . that never knew body." And lastly, in the culminating *fanā'* (death to this life), the essence of the creature disappears in the light of the divine essence, like stars in sunlight, so the Lord is visible, the servant invisible. There are specific passages in al-Fāriḍ's *Tā'iyyat* which correspond very closely to the final two verse paragraphs of "Albae Meditatio," but I will not reproduce them here; the interested reader can find them in the Loloi article or in Nicholson's *Studies in Islamic Mysticism*.

In the penultimate verse paragraph of "Albae Meditatio," the Beloved finally "unveils herself," and the narrator-poet lets go of final reservations and defenses against her power over him. The law of Love and the Muses makes different demands than does the law on Sinai, the Mosaic law; this accounts for the "Thou shalt not!" the poet asks of her—and a wordplay on "Muses" and "Moses" reinforces this dynamic. In the erotic and spiritual union the lover seeks with the Beloved, vision itself will be superseded, since "once united with thee [man] no more needs to see"—this state is what the mystics call "the Second Separation" where "even Sinai is laid low."

13. Nicholson, *Studies in Islamic Mysticism*, 241–42.

Nicholson in his commentary on al-Fāriḍ explains what is meant by this. In the first separation the mystic is still conscious of himself or herself as an individual. We recognize this state in the opening lines of "Albae Meditatio," where reference is made to the poet's "fallacious eye" from which the indwelling Spirit is "hidden everywhere." This separation is surmounted through the ecstatic state often referred to as intoxication, where the devotee is conscious of nothing but God, whose "very veils are Revelation itself." According to al-Fāriḍ, however, the supreme state of oneness is not intoxication, but rather "sobriety" or the return to consciousness, "the second separation," when, in Nicholson's words, "the mystic (who in the former 'separation' knew himself as 'other than God') knows himself as the subject and object of all action, and perceives that 'union' and 'separation' are the same thing seen from different points of view."[14] The poem begins and ends, then, in paradox. From "Her very veils are Revelation itself," we come to the separation that is union. This corresponds to Meister Eckhart's teaching that to long for union with God constitutes an obstacle to that very union; ultimate surrender confounds the will of the spiritual seeker, who nevertheless is bound to seek God. This state is represented by Russell in the final stanza as a beautiful young woman who seduces the old man's dissolute body. Not surprisingly, given what we have already encountered in the poem, the ultimate union is represented by the *coincidentia oppositorum*— "O holy saeculum, and O unholy heavens," and the Solomonic Wisdom is a "wanton harlot." Certainly the poet's outcry in the final lines of the poem, "Open with all your awful revelations! / I am here," is a facing of literal death as well as a spiritual one. We note that Russell wrote this poem when he was seventy years old, isolated and quite penniless. In his final decade he wrote many poems about the humbling experience of bodily decrepitude.

Russell added the closing words, "and I am She" (importantly, without a period, and thus refusing closure even here), some time after the poem's original composition date. It was a brilliant move: the final touch the poem was waiting for, with its original, very briefly mentioned state of suspension in the final line, "I am here." Russell gives a key to the meaning of "I am She" with a footnote at the bottom of the page: "Cf. 'Ed io son ella', Cecco d'Ascoli *c.* 1300 also Ibn Fârid, *c.* 1220 ('anà hia')."[15]

Cecco d'Ascoli (1269–1327), an almost exact contemporary of Dante, was an astrologer and professor in Bologna who was burned at the stake

14. Nicholson, *Studies in Islamic Mysticism*, 224.

15. Russell, *Poesie dal Valdarno*, 79.

for heresy in Florence. He is best known for his long encyclopedic poem, *Acerba*. Cecco was scandalized by Dante's by-passing of the unique status of the Virgin Mary and his creation of an alternative woman holy guide in Beatrice; in short, he did not believe that actual women were capable of the subtle thoughts expressed by Beatrice in the *Divine Comedy* (where she, for example, corrects the views even of Thomas Aquinas). For instance, in a misogynistic passage in *Acerba*, Cecco would write: "Maria si va cercando per Ravenna / Chi in donna crede che sia intelletto": "He who believes that there is an intellect in woman goes searching for Mary in Ravenna [i.e., he will never find her there]"; and he elsewhere clarifies that the Virgin Mary alone among actual women possessed intellect. Needless to say, this completely contradicts what Dante represents in most of his writing, where actual living women, especially Beatrice, are the bearers of divine wisdom. Cecco aims in *Acerba* to refute and correct Dante's heterodox views.

The purely spiritual figure of Sapientia, or Wisdom, on the other hand, represented by Cecco as the Phoenix, is the beloved who represents the active intelligence that illuminates the receptive soul. She is the one Cecco is referring to where he writes the phrase, "Dunque, io son ella" (which Russell slightly misquotes) in *Acerba*. Russell seems unaware of the dualism inherent in Cecco's approach to the archetypal feminine, compared to Dante's greater integration of human love and divine love. Nevertheless, Cecco's phrase for Russell expresses the conjunction of masculine and feminine, the fusion of the active intellect with matter or form; and in "The Figure of Woman" Russell refers it to the medieval-scholastic symbolism of sexual union—the so-called *copulatio* or *connubium*—where the possible intellect "dies" into the universal Intellect. This is one area of the background to the final phrase of "Albae Meditatio." As for al-Fāriḍ, the phrase "I am She" appears twice in the *Tā'iyyat*: "I was ever She, and She was ever I, with no difference: nay, my essence loved my essence"; and: "If I recant my words, I am She, or if I say far be it from one like me to say it! that She became incarnate in me, (then I shall deserve to die the death)." Russell concludes in his essay: "Plainly, 'She' is God or the Self. In Persian *khud* means self, and is used as the reflexive pronoun and the emphatic, like *se* and *ipse* in Latin. But *khudā* means God. *Khudā* in modern Persian in fact is derived from *khudāgā*—knowing God, or 'coming from God.'"[16]

In my interview with Russell, he recounted a dream that he had had six months earlier, which might be seen as an alternative narrative of the

---

16. Russell, "Figure of Woman," in *Image of Woman*, 90.

themes expressed in "Albae Meditatio." I would like to conclude my essay with this dream as told in Russell's own words, in part because lucid dreams are closer to poetry than critical prose is, and in part because this particular dream gives the entire interpretation of the poem, as it were, in a stroke. I was impressed not only by the dream itself but by its testimony to the fullness and passion with which Russell lived his poetry and brought poetry to his life.

> I had an amazing dream, in which I was Quintilius [a fictional Silver Age Latin poet, Russell's persona in an ongoing series of poems], with my queen of the Indian estate that I ruled successfully for many years, and we left the estate to our children and retired to the forest in traditional Brahman style. It was a pilgrimage that we'd been making for many years. And we thought we were doing fine; we thought we'd freed ourselves of the ego and we were living completely in the spirit. At a certain point, we come up against what is a *huge* wall—you know, imagine a wall that is fifty meters high or a hundred meters high. With great stones mortared together. We go round and round and round, there's no gate in it at all, and we just sort of lie down and weep. No way to get in. Obviously this is the wall around Paradise. Nirvana. At a certain point, a young Buddhist monk comes, and he gives us a sweet smile, and *he just walks through the wall*. It was the most wonderful dream. Later, the monk came back and helped us a great deal, and we got inside. The inside . . . I mean, I couldn't express in words how beautiful it was. Super-reality.

In our discussion about the dream, I commented on its obvious allusion to death, and Russell added:

> I'm not depressed about death, but the thing about death that makes me sad is that I can't go on with the work I'm doing. But of course that is a form of egoism. That's why I can't get into the Garden. You can't have it both ways. You can't have your cake and eat it. And you've got to give up one or the other. That dream was unbelievable. I've never seen such . . . you could see *every* leaf, every serration on every leaf, *wonderful colors*, birds of every color and shape, singing—marvelously.

As in "Albae Meditatio," a radiant natural setting, with birdsong prominent once again, is the place where a love union occurs that is an enactment of self-transcendence, and where death of the self and literal death are virtually indistinguishable.

Touching the World

The Ascetic Art of John Haines

J OHN Haines was well known in his lifetime as a poet who commu-
nicated, not only his experience of homesteading in Alaska, but also
a view of modern industrial and postindustrial society as seen from
the perspective he gained during his years in the wilderness. Ever since I
discovered Haines's poetry in an anthology years ago, I've returned to it
many times for its sanity, intensity, and focus. After reading his various
poetry collections, starting with his debut volume *Winter News* (1966) and
through his *New Poems, 1980–88* (1990) and his collected poems, *The Owl
in the Mask of the Dreamer* (1993), I turned to his prose memoirs *The Stars,
the Snow, the Fire: Twenty-five Years in the Northern Wilderness* (1989) and
Living off the Country: Essays on Poetry and Place (1981). All of Haines's
work draws on his economical, vivid depictions of hunting, trapping,
building, and surviving in Alaska, at the Richardson homestead north of
Fairbanks, where Haines lived on and off for twenty-five years. He seems to
know every feature, habit, and use of the land and the plants and animals
around him.

I met John Haines in person once, after we'd exchanged letters for a few
years, when he was a fellow at the Rockefeller Foundation Bellagio Center
on Lake Como in the fall of 2000. Haines by then was an old man, but as we
and his wife, Joy, and mine, Daphne, strolled about the grounds of the villa
that once belonged to Pliny the Younger, he was like a boy fascinated by the
natural features around us. He commented on things many would over-
look, pausing to appreciate the mushrooms and other flora. I was struck by
how alert and present he was to the minutiae of the natural world.

One passage in *The Stars, the Snow, the Fire* that stood out for me is, "In this wilderness life I have found a way to touch the world once more. . . . I relive each day the ancient expectation of the hunt—the setting out, and the trail at dawn."[1] Indeed, Haines's knowledge of nature is realistic, detailed, and practical, even as it is also matter for poetry and prose. In his writing, naturalism blends with an appreciation of nature as the signature of all things, a nonverbal language that Haines attempts to put into words. The point of contact between mind and world is especially palpable in Haines's prose, where that world also touches the reader through the transparent medium the poet has crafted. There is a speaker, but he only speaks when necessary or useful, and he is also a good listener—not often a listener to people, but, important as well, a listener to the rhythms of the wilderness. Haines's words are stamped with the reality of the creatures and things he lived with so closely.

Of course, Haines could have gone to Alaska and homesteaded without writing about it. What was the relation between his practice of writing and his experience of touching the world? Only he, if anyone, could have answered that question, but it is clear that Haines, like everyone dedicated to the craft of poetry, felt a need not just to survive in the wilderness but to create himself. There is a wilderness of the mind as well, and Haines explored that as a kind of microcosm of the Alaskan subarctic. His life in Alaska gave him images for the expansive, sometimes fecund and sometimes desolate spaces of the contemplative and reflective mind. In his later poetry, from the late 1970s on, Haines looked at society and culture in terms of both wildernesses, outer and inner, as in the poem "In the Forest Without Leaves," from *New Poems*:

> I have looked back across
> the waste of numerals—
> each tortured geometry
> of township and lot—
>
> to the round and roadless vista,
> to the wind-furrow
> in the forest track
> when I had myself entire.[2]

1. Haines, *The Stars*, 83.

2. Except for one quotation from Haines's last collection, *For the Century's End*, all quotations from his poetry are taken from *Owl in the Mask of the Dreamer*, which is his *Collected Poems* up until 1993.

As this excerpt shows, Haines's literary technique and style reflects the spare, unadorned life of the homesteader: brief lyrics, or sequences of brief lyrics, composed of two- to four-beat lines, syntactically simple, unflinchingly sober and still. It is the poetic equivalent of the moccasins or dog harnesses that Haines put together with strips of moose hide. They are the verses of a taciturn man, living in a country where there are few women. It is a severe view in many ways, a secular asceticism, and the language of Haines's poetry is pared down, layer by layer and veil by veil, to the essentials. It is a voice that knows the bare necessities of life with brutal directness, and does not want to waste words, for fear they will only ring hollow.

A key to Haines's sense that setting aside modern life's complexities and distractions had enabled him to touch the world is that he simply paid attention. The naturalistic detail in his writing is always intimate and clear, perceived with an alert and humble presence of mind. His compressed style suggests something similar to the practice of meditation, where thoughts and sensations are slowed in a narrow sluice of attention. Chinese and Japanese poetry in translation had a formative influence on Haines's style. Japanese literary tradition, going back at least to the twelfth century, refers to the *hon'i* of a poetic subject, which is its essence or primordial substance. In order to reveal *hon'i*, the poet had to focus attention, not on superficial aspects of the poetic topic, but on the essence of the topic as it lay within the poet's own mind. The poet had to become one with the subject in order to disclose its being. Clearly the conditions of contemporary society make it very hard indeed for anyone to find such receptive focus. Haines found it not only by leaving all the distractions behind, but by finding language that corresponded to his discovery. When he says that he finally touched the world, he is also saying, since he is a poet, that he has found something to say about its interior reality, and that this reality is inseparable from himself.

A moment's thought reveals that contemplation speaks many languages. We have only to consider such diverse writers as Henry David Thoreau, Gerard Manley Hopkins, and William Everson to see how expressions of oneness are multiple—in imagery, style, and rhythms adapted to the author's temperament. Haines's experience of nature was more savage, more tied to survival, than it was for any of these writers, and the poetry he discovered in it is correspondingly severe in its beauty. One of his most remarkable poems, "Meditation on a Skull Carved in Crystal," published in *New Poems*, approaches a stillness that verges on an agnostic *via negativa:*

Intelligence is what we find,
gazing into rock as into water
at the same depth shining.

Mirror, glazed forehead of snow.
Holes for its eyes, to see
what the dead see dying:

a grain of ice in the stellar
blackness, lighted
by a sun, distant within.

While a writer like Hopkins, in his journals and his poetry, used the surface qualities of language to create energy and motion like electromagnetic fields—his so-called sprung rhythms, each with their own texture—Haines aimed for transparency, the limpid surface, a steady calm of perception. The arctic air of Alaska had contracted his language and thought to their austere essentials.

Having submitted himself to nature's teachings, when Haines returned to the mainland United States in 1969 he found his vocation as spokesman for an easily forgotten truth: that nature is the ever-present backdrop and foundation of culture. As Dana Gioia wrote in his introduction to Haines's *New Poems*, "The special splendor of Haines's poetry is that it honors experience without cheating literature. He mastered the craft of poetry without forgetting that art both originates and returns to life."[3] In Haines's later poems, such as the following lines from the final poem in *The Owl in the Mask of the Dreamer*, there are occasional echoes of King James Bible language—probably, since Haines did not read the Bible when he was young (as he told me in a letter), coming to him through his reading of English poets:

Divided is the man of hidden
purpose, and evil his redemption.

Harness the wind and drive the water,
you that govern,
who yoke and stride the world . . . ("Night")

3. This essay, which originally was the introduction to *New Poems*, is reprinted in an anthology of essays about Haines's work: Bezner and Walzer, *The Wilderness of Vision*, 182–89.

Such traces of English prophetic language and other landmarks of the tradition are pervasive in Haines's later work. There is something profoundly western about Haines's position, however much the calm surface of his language derives from his reading of Ezra Pound's and Kenneth Rexroth's translations of Chinese and Japanese poetry. One often notes an ornery intellectual skepticism, more like Diogenes the Cynic (a persona Haines explicitly adopted for some of his last poems) than Li Po. George Santayana in *Three Philosophical Poets*, a book that Haines admired, sketches the basic trends of the western philosophical tradition as they are typified by three great poets. Santayana designates Lucretius as the poet of naturalism; Dante as the poet of supernaturalism; and Goethe (in relation to *Faust*) as the quintessential romantic poet of "mystical faith in will and action." This description of Goethe clearly fits Haines's forging of a life in the wilderness and the courage required to follow such a calling—as in fact it describes the American pioneering spirit in general.

The other two traditions, of which Lucretius and Dante are the supreme poetic exemplars, also shed light on the worldview implicit in Haines's writing. Lucretius wrote *De rerum natura* (On the Nature of Things) partly to present nature shorn of its anthropomorphism or to debunk the notion that humanity is somehow special within the natural scheme of things. We too will perish, like all things natural, says Lucretius; our bodies come from nature and will decay back into it. Anyone who has read Haines knows that he has much to say along these lines. How could he not, with his daily experiences of death, killing, and the necessities of survival? "A drowsy, half-wakeful menace waits for us in the quietness of the world," he writes in *The Stars, the Snow, the Fire*. "I was suddenly aware of something that did not care if I lived."[4] The critic Carolyn J. Allen's essay "Death and Dreams in John Haines's *Winter News*" analyzes Haines's use of images of whiteness and snow to evoke an image of death.[5] She is right: death is everywhere in Haines's poetry. Even in the later poems, the reader constantly encounters an urge to see life, phenomena, and the artifacts of social life through to their conclusion in demise, death, silence, and entropy. Like Lucretius, Haines is profoundly aware of nature's engulfing impersonality. *The Owl in the Mask of the Dreamer* and *The Stars, the Snow, the Fire* both finish with images of dissolution and vast darkness.

4. Haines, *The Stars*, 95.
5. This essay can be found in Bezner and Walzer, *Wilderness of Vision*, 145–54.

Leave to me
this one sustaining solace—

my night that has more night
to come. ("Night")

The man turns away, pulling his parka hood around him. He walks again on the road in the direction he came from, into the wind, toward Tenderfoot Hill. He disappears in the darkness. Snow closes around him, filling his tracks as he goes. ("Richardson: The Dream")[6]

But the very restlessness for and impetus toward emptiness and night in Haines betrays his affinity also with the spiritual view that Santayana examines in Dante. A fundamental characteristic of that view, Santayana says, is that "its sources are in the solitude of the spirit and in the disparity, or the opposition, between what the spirit feels it is fitted to do, and what, in this world, it is condemned to waste itself upon."[7] The image of death that we find in Haines is related to a spirituality that aims to tear away the non-essential, knowing it won't last—rending the veils, seeking all or nothing. It is a passion to reach the life that external life easily forgets or glosses over. The classical-naturalistic view represented by Lucretius, on the other hand, comes up with a different conclusion, based on the same fundamental observation of nature's sublime disregard for individual existence. Seeing the eventual dissolution of all creatures and things, that view prescribes that our brief span of life should be lived in bodily fullness and respect for the great forces of nature.

One way to see Haines's writing, then, is that it inhabits a space between spiritual faith or longing and a realism learned firsthand in the most basic of material circumstances. Haines does not write explicitly from any one religious or cosmological tradition, although (as he also told me in a letter) he did once consider the Catholic priesthood, and it is clear that religiosity in a broad sense informs much of what he writes. He makes frequent, eclectic use of myths and fables from a variety of sources. Haines felt a special affinity with the Scottish poet Edwin Muir, and wrote the introduction to the Graywolf edition of Muir's essays *The Estate of Poetry*. Muir's

6. Haines, *The Stars*, 162.
7. Santayana, *Three Philosophical Poets*, 6–7.

imagination, like Haines's, was deeply informed by the natural world he knew and loved—for Muir, the seascape of the Orkneys and the farm life of his family and community. And although Muir wrote explicitly from a Christian-Platonist viewpoint, while Haines did not, Haines as much as Muir wrote out of a need to create a *fable* to go with the *story* of his life. The "fable" is our life seen from the side of the dreaming mind or imagination; in it and through it, the particulars of our lives tell a universal story. For Haines, "touching the world" was made possible by living as he did in the wilderness and finding a way to write the fable of that experience.

"The Legend," a poem in Haines's last full collection of poetry, *For the Century's End* (2001), uses the ancient story of Gilgamesh to depict a mythical alienation from nature parallel to the expulsion from Eden, a favorite topic of Muir. For both writers, the theme of paradise found and lost is the essence of their "fables." In *Gilgamesh*, the main character, who is the king of Uruk, and his friend Enkidu, who comes from the wilds where he grazed and drank with the animals, together kill a bull sent by the gods, for which they suffer divine retribution. Haines's lecture "The Theme of Loss, of Sorrow and Redemption in *Gilgamesh*," given in the late 1990s, discusses his intimate relationship with the Gilgamesh story.[8] As he says at the start of that lecture, "When, [after his homesteading years] . . . I first read a translation of *Gilgamesh*, I knew that in some way I was reading of my own life. . . . [*Gilgamesh* is about] transgression against the forest gods, of punishment, and eventual reconciliation"—the very theme that permeates Haines's writing. Haines's work communicates not only the touch of the world as he came to know it in his life in the wilderness, but also, inevitably, the loss of that touch, the exile from unity.

One of the things that made Haines an unusual writer in the modern world is that he profoundly *experienced* this unity or touch of the world; it was one of the formative experiences of his life. It is an experience which most of us need to be reminded is possible, since it is so difficult to find in the context of the hypertechnological contemporary world. One source of the unrest and widespread sociopathy of our time may be that many people are not aware that we are in exile or that there is any state of mind or nature to be in exile *from*; as if the state of alienation and division are the inevitable, one-sided norm. A writer like Haines shows us otherwise. As he writes in *The Stars, the Snow, the Fire*: "It was far, far back in time,

8. I have seen this piece only in the typed copy the author sent to me, which I still have.

that twilight country where men sometimes lose their way, become as trees confused in the shapes of snow. But I was at home there, my mind bent away from humanity, to learn to think a little like that thing I was hunting."[9] As he says in the Gilgamesh poem mentioned above: "I know the name of that exile, / . . . the parting and breaking of things." In his lecture on the Gilgamesh epic he says: "In leaving that wilderness life behind, as I did at the end of the 1960s, I could not have defined my reasons for doing so. I knew that a certain life in a loved place had mysteriously come to an end."[10] That he found a way to write about his experience of paradise found and paradise lost, touch and isolation, unity and division, was a singular contribution to American letters.

9. Haines, *The Stars*, 28.
10. Haines, "Theme of Loss," 5.

Richard Berengarten's Blue Butterfly

THE English poet Richard Berengarten (formerly Burns, before he returned to his family name) is not as widely known as he might be, based on his literary achievement—a situation for which I can think of a couple of reasons. First, Berengarten's book publications, which go back to the late 1960s, have been mostly with small presses and so have not been widely available or publicized. Salt Publications tried to do something about that in the 2000s: *For the Living* (2004), a selection of Berengarten's longer poems from 1965 to 2000, was the first in a series of his writings to be issued by Salt. *The Blue Butterfly* and *In a Time of Drought*, the first two volumes of his *Balkan Trilogy*, were published by Salt in 2006, and the third volume, *Under Balkan Light*, came out in 2008.[1] A few years later *The Salt Companion to Richard Berengarten*, edited by Norman Jope, presented more than 450 pages of prose about Berengarten's work by various poets, critics, and scholars. The Salt editions of Berengarten went out of print, but were subsequently brought out by Shearsmans Books. Since 2015, Berengarten has also published a couple of new poetry collections with Shearsmans, including *Notness*, a series of one hundred metaphysical sonnets (the title is an anagram of the word *sonnets*) that Berengarten composed between 1967 and 2013. And in 2021, *Balkan Spaces*, a prose book of essays and sketches to complement his *Balkan Trilogy*, was issued by that publisher.

---

1. Berengarten lived in the former Yugoslavia in the late 1980s and early 1990s and his daughter was born in Belgrade, so the Balkans have much personal and poetic significance for him.

Another reason that Berengarten is not as widely known as his achievement merits may be his frequent use of hermetic and archetypal thought and symbolism in his poetry, areas which are outside the spectrum of most contemporary literature and criticism. His 1972 collection *Avebury*, for example, articulated a foundation myth in terms adapted to the postmodern perspective—a time when, writes Berengarten, responding to Yeats's phrase "the centre will not hold," the centre is "every / where." Berengarten has written on ambitious and far-reaching themes without the conceptual distancing, limiting confessionalism, or ironical disclaimers that are common in contemporary poetry. Yet he also writes as someone totally engaged with the world as it is, openly grappling with present-day cultural uprootedness and disorientation. Berengarten's book-length sequence *The Manager* (2001) is an extended dramatic monologue of an executive in a multinational corporation, interrupted occasionally by other "voices." This fiction gave Berengarten a means for exploring current idioms and jargon, as well as contemporary dissociated mental states. It is the first of Berengarten's books that I read, and I was so impressed by the vitality and inventiveness of the language that I wanted to follow it up with more by him.

Which brings me to Berengarten's collection *The Blue Butterfly*, a book-length sequence about the massacre of thousands of Serbians by the Nazis in World War II. Composed between May 1985 and April 2006, the book's conception came about when the author was visiting Šumarice, in the former Yugoslavia (now central-western Serbia), where a museum commemorates the massacre carried out by the Nazis on October 19–21, 1941, six months after the Nazi invasion of Yugoslavia. Šumarice is an area just outside Kragujevac, which is the main city of that part of Serbia. Berengarten explains that while he and his daughter were waiting to enter the museum, a blue butterfly came to rest on the forefinger of his left hand, which is the hand he writes with. They each took photographs of the butterfly, one of which is shown in the book's frontispiece.

The title poem and one other poem were written—or wrote themselves, as he says—immediately after his return to England. I will quote the book's eponymous poem in full, since it expresses so clearly the moral energy that led Berengarten to pursue a project that took him twenty years to complete:

> On my Jew's hand, born out of ghettos and shtetls,
> raised from unmarked graves of my obliterated people
> in Germany, Latvia, Lithuania, Poland, Russia,

on my hand mothered by a refugee's daughter,
first opened in blitzed London, grown big
through post-war years safe in suburban England,

on my pink, educated, ironical left hand
of a parvenu not quite British pseudo gentleman
which first learned to scrawl its untutored messages

among Latin-reading rugby-playing militarists
in an élite boarding school on Sussex's green downs
and against the cloister walls of puritan Cambridge,

on my hand weakened by anomie, on my
writing hand, now of a sudden willingly
stretched before me in Serbian spring sunlight,

on my unique living hand, trembling and troubled
by this May visitation, like a virginal
leaf new sprung on the oldest oak in Europe,

on my proud firm hand, miraculously blessed
by the two thousand eight hundred martyred
men, women and children fallen at Kragujevac,

a blue butterfly simply fell out of the sky
and settled on the forefinger
of my international bloody human hand.[2]

After the writing of this poem and the one that follows it in the collection, entitled "Nada: Hope or Nothing," Berengarten set out to study the history of World War II in the former Yugoslavia and of the massacre that took place at Šumarice. The fruits of this study are evident in the book's postscript, which documents the historical background, and in the notes section. While Berengarten was living in Yugoslavia, he planned the book's structure and composed early drafts of many of its poems.

George Szirtes has called *The Blue Butterfly* an "epic," but for me the word epic is too elevated or heroic for what the collection contains. I prefer to think of it as an extended meditation: on tragedy, on the dead, on beauty and ugliness, on good and evil. *The Blue Butterfly* is a commemoration, as Szirtes also says; it is a generous foray into ritualized grief, dismay, and

2. All quotations from Berengarten's poetry are from *The Blue Butterfly*.

wonder. It is a richly conceived, integrated sequence, beginning in darkness and consternation, undergoing the *katabasis* of existential doubt and despair, and ending with affirmation.

Berengarten clearly gave much thought to the book's design. There are seven sections of seven poems each. Berengarten has often employed number symbolism, one of the ways in which he utilizes hermetic thought in his work. For example, his book of sonnets mentioned earlier, *Notness*, is composed of ten sections of ten sonnets each. His long poem *Tree* (1980), which is about the kabbalistic tree of life as well as physical trees, has the same number of lines, 365, as a calendar year has days. Berengarten's choice of the number seven for *The Blue Butterfly* would also seem to be related to his Jewish ancestry (his father was an immigrant to London from Warsaw). Seven is a sacred number in many traditions, but I am going to hazard a guess that Berengarten is using the number seven here as an analog of the Sabbath, the day of rest that commemorates the seventh day of the creation, on which, Genesis says, God rested because the creation was complete and good. Seven in this sense is the number of the wholeness that blesses— which is how *The Blue Butterfly* ends, with seven "blessings" of the lives that were desecrated by the massacre.

Very little of the poetry in this book directly recalls the terrible event itself; the documentation at the end, which includes old photographs, serves that function. One poem at the start of the book records the Nazi order to carry out the murder of one hundred Serbs for every German soldier killed by Serbian insurgents, and fifty Serbs for every wounded German. This poem, called "Two Documents," is a dark satire on officialese—the language this poem imitates—which expresses the oft-noted dullness of the Nazi mindset, what Hannah Arendt referred to as the banality of evil, of totalitarianism driven by monotonous monomaniacal efficiency.[3] As Berengarten's poem puts it: "The quick / and ruthless suppression of the Serbian uprising // represents a considerable gain towards the final / German Victory." The next poem narrates matter-of-factly the day of the massacre, interspersed with quotations from notes the victims wrote to loved ones just before they were taken to slaughter—a few of the notes are reproduced in the documentary section of the book.

And that is all, in terms of direct, specific reference to the atrocity. The remainder of the book is alternately a commemoration of the victims and a self-reflective exploration of the fact of being a poet-survivor of this and

---

3. Arendt, *Eichmann in Jerusalem.*

other holocausts (again, Berengarten's ancestry clearly is important here). All of us, as survivors, are left to confront or avoid or gloss over the darkest nadirs of our history, where "lie sentences so deep they are unsayable." And yet, as a poet, Berengarten is compelled to try to say the unsayable. In "The Telling," which is a poem in three "attempts," as Berengarten calls them, the poet asks: "Is it *language itself* won't do here?" His hope is

> to carry a cargo of such immense weight
> of souls from the hold of their burying ground,
> seal pain, refine death, transubstantiate
> blood, to wine, to spirit. This, blue fritillary,
> flight filtered fine in a poem's distillery,
> is how I would ring their memorial sound.

And yet, to do this is to confront a paradox: how can the poet craft an aesthetic object based on a tragedy that appears so unredeemable and unspeakable? As the mother of a dead child says in a sequence of seven villanelles called "The Death of Children":

> There is no comfort. What comfort can come,
> when neither here nor up on high
> are love and justice more than martyrdom?

Furthermore, what do we, the living, do with the fact of the world's beauty, of our pleasure or happiness on a given day, given the stain on our memory brought about by tragedies like the one in Ŝumarice?

> The mental stench of soil soaked in spilt blood
> drowns out even the blueness of this heaven.

A poem from "Seven Wreaths," a sonnet sequence that takes as its starting point the flowers that have grown where the massacre took place, asks, "Could flowers' quiet voices avenge these fallen?" But how can nature heal anything, when, as the father of a dead child puts it, "Bloody in vengeance, red in tooth and claw," nature is so often a force that "snarl[s] at human longing, love and law"? On one hand, Berengarten's view of regeneration echoes Shelley in its use of natural imagery to depict an eschatological redemption:

> Should ever judgement come to fit this crime,
> should these dead but awaken, and their tombs
> throw up their burdens, in that timeless time
> when earth harvests redemption, then these blooms

will rise with scaly wings, like imagos
of butterflies, blue heralds . . .

and, again echoing Shelley's "Ode to the West Wind":

Rooted in death, but death's antithesis,
what is this wreath, if not hope's chrysalis?

—even if, for now, the flowers the speaker is observing are merely "weak angels, harbingers . . . / in blood and crimson rose." The red of the flowers, lovely to look at, is also a reminder of blood. The shedding of blood almost always leads to more shedding of blood. Once again, the poet resolves this dilemma by an imaginative leap: "until / red stands for more than . . . avenging will," and "until revenge'll / take vengeance on itself, take eye for eye / no more."

In the above quotations, Berengarten writes in the tradition that stakes a claim for imagination's practical efficacy. But this optimism is tempered in the next sonnet: "Against revenge? No. Just a mass of flowers." Similarly, elsewhere he writes that "the dead do not hear us, and we are not Orpheus"; and "how / can the likes of us claim anywhere anything more / than a handful of smoke and puff or wisp of dust?"; and "I should like to speak with conviction but am condemned / to stammering." Further, he asks, can it be that

everything we have been vanishes
and consciousness itself of what we have been vanishes
and all we have imagined, believed, dreamed and aspired to,
even touched and reached, really consisted of nothing?

In such passages, and there are many in this collection and elsewhere in Berengarten's work, we find ourselves in the area of postmodern doubt. Berengarten has been consistent in being a romantic who shares in the existential angst and epistemological uncertainties of the present. Holding to seemingly contrary opposites—not even settling on "antifoundationalism" and other poststructural gerbil wheels—he practices negative capability in its original, Keatsian sense. In his prose, Berengarten has expressed his debt to the Jungian James Hillman, who advocated just such an approach, in books such as *The Dream and the Underworld*, which seems directly to inform parts of the longest poem in *The Blue Butterfly*, "Conversation Between a Blue Butterfly and a Murdered Man at One of the Entrances to the Underworld." This poem is one of the pieces in "Flight of the Imago," the most philosophical section in this book, in which the author ruminates in long, metrically loose lines. Hillman was consistent in his defense of the soul's perspective, which he contrasted with that of the spirit.[4] The spirit, said Hillman, is azure-inclined, arrowlike in its trajectory, ascetic, and detached. The soul, meanwhile, enjoys dark depths, attachments, and ambiguity. While the spirit soars the soul flits—hence its name in Greek, *psyche*, butterfly. This is no doubt why the blue butterfly is the muse of this book: "Teach me, blue butterfly, to open / these winged words in singing and in dancing." That an actual blue butterfly landed on the author's physical hand does not preclude its being a symbol as well. This is the meaning of synchronicity, which Jung said is an "acausal connecting principle" behind meaningful coincidences.[5] This way of thinking is consistent with hermetic or orphic thought, which doesn't explain relations between events in terms of cause and effect but rather by analogy. Synchronicity is the theory of correspondences ("As above so below") in practice.

In a long dialogue between the blue butterfly and a man murdered by the Nazis, the butterfly acts as Mercurial psychopomp, or soul-guide, explaining that "Language has gaps and holes and in them lurk / many incomprehensible expanses." But for Berengarten, as for Hillman, these gaps are entrances to another kind of consciousness, however disorienting—an underworld awareness that is totally ungraspable by reason, not just the dead end of nihil, as in so much postmodernese. The murdered man asks the butterfly: "*Into or out of what notness do you call me?*" to which the butterfly responds, "Where but under dark. Underneath it. Under / Death"—a response that goes back at least to Heraclitus.[6]

Like any contemporary writer, Berengarten has at his disposal fewer collectively recognizable symbols and images than premoderns had for writing about evil and death. Dante had all of hell to work with, guided by the moral philosophy of Cicero, Aristotle, and Thomas Aquinas. The Hindus had their pantheon of demons, the Greeks their Furies and fickle gods. Twenty-first-century culture doesn't have the shared symbolic language for

---

4. See Hillman, "Excursion on Differences Between Soul and Spirit," in *Re-Visioning Psychology*, 67–70.

5. Jung, *Synchronicity*.

6. Heraclitus, Fragment 42: "You could not discover the limits of soul, even if you traveled by every path in order to do so; such is the depth of its meaning" (Wheelwright, *The Presocratics*, 72). Hillman comments on this fragment: "Soul is not in the surface of things, the superficialities, but reaches down into hidden depths, a region which also refers to Hades and death" (*Re-Visioning Psychology*, 231 n. 6).

giving shape to archetypal experience, so we are left for the most part with existential reflections and private or eclectic symbols, or perhaps with writing for a coterie of believers. So, Berengarten concludes:

> Whoever offers arguments pretends
> to read fate's lines. Although we must swear by
> what justice is, nobody comprehends
>
> how destiny of chance weaves.[7]

Likewise, in a poem about a woman mourning a loved one, the poet says,

> She does not believe
> in God, yet to the dead human, god-huge in her head,
> she ferries wordless questions.

And what are we to make of the apparent randomness of fate? "What hand, against the odds, pulled the Warsavian / musician out of the queue from ghetto to gas chamber . . . Why him and not another?"; and "The detached Goddess *Ananke* [a goddess of fate or necessity] pours acid on our eyes / and smiles the far-away smile of a lover, thug / or torturer." Given this brutal indifference of life, what is the point of poetry—or as one poem title says, "What Then Is Singing? And What Dancing?" Berengarten's answer is that it is

> an emptying and replenishing
> of the full cup of memory, into now and always
> from the source of always and now

by which we

> transform petty purpose into total celebration
> of now in the cup of always, always in the bowl of now.

Berengarten's response to totalizing death and negation is that, despite the unchanging predictable routineness of evil and human stupidity, "we must love"—love and courage extend beyond our individual lives or collective present, "to thread . . . through the fibres of the tree / that outspans and outlasts our histories." As another poem puts it:

---

7. Berengarten has acknowledged in a private communication that the image of reading "fate's lines" is consciously derived from the *I Ching*.

> I affirm still a man may trace his particular vision
> however vicarious or wavering, like the path
> of a blue butterfly
> . . .
>
> . . . register that, for always, in memory's palpable zone
> for anybody who comes there, everybody who comes there,
> to visit, to be touched by beauty, as one enters a garden.

One of the outstanding poems in *The Blue Butterfly* is a dream-vision narrative in terza rima. It appears in a section of "Seven Statements of Survivors"—and, again, it is clear that by "survivors" Berengarten means all of us. In this poem, the narrator encounters a goddess or anima figure by the sea. The sun has just passed beneath the horizon; it is dusk. The feminine figure, whose "silhouetted body might stir love's / unrealised longings in me, yet be bearable," comes to the narrator "as if she knew my self-esteem // had sunk so deep, I had lost hope." She represents the transformative power of beauty; in this case, given the darkness of the book's subject, beauty that is met on the other side of "the deepest terrors you must face." She is an initiator: "call me keeper of that door // locked fast below fear's last extremity"; "Your soul is summoned to the secret source of day," where the sun has gone, below the horizon. Indeed, the structure of *The Blue Butterfly* as a whole could be seen as an enactment of the sun's journey at night, renewal through descent.[8] Or, as one of the massacre victim-narrators in "Seven Songs of the Dead" puts it, addressing his daughter who is mourning him at his grave:

> when your dusk closes
> and your sun fails
> the black suns on my scales
> guide me through mazes
> unthreaded by cock-crow.

and in another poem:

> The black light behind the sun
> opens. And on the skies, black stars.

The Blue Butterfly as a whole is both troubling and consolatory, because the author's response to his difficult subject is complex, imaginative,

---

8. The same motif occurs in others writings by Berengarten. See, e.g., his study of the sun symbolism in Ceri Richards's painting *The Black Apple of Gower*, in *Ceri Richards and Dylan Thomas*, 72–73, 75–78.

and unsentimental. Richard Berengarten has been doing this sort of important work for decades, through his numerous publications. He speaks to us with a fullness and range that our collective historical moment calls for.

DAVID MASON AND THE HUMAN PLACE

STARTING with his earliest collection, *The Buried Houses* (1991), David Mason has made poetry out of his family roots. Mason grew up in Washington state but his ancestors were from Colorado, which is where Mason lived and taught for many years (until he moved to Tasmania with his wife, a native Tasmanian—we will return to this later). His verse novel *Ludlow* (2007) is a dramatization of the Colorado coal miners' strike in 1913–14 and of the massacre of strikers and their family members by the coal company's hired thugs and the state militia. As Mason explains in the afterword to that book, the idea for writing the Ludlow story had been in him since he was a boy visiting the area with his family: "What excited me about this story was not any political agenda, but the elements that have always obsessed me—family, landscape, immigration, language."[1] Or, as he puts it in a narrator's aside in *Ludlow*: "this story hooks into desires / I've always felt to know the land I come from."[2]

Mason's writing often suggests something along the lines of what Wendell Berry has called accepting a place properly human in the world as it is. As Berry puts it, place is a form the way a sonnet is a form; we work within the limits it sets, and if we are skillful, patient, and lucky enough we give it new life. Mason's collection *Arrivals* (2004) opens with a version of Cavafy's poem "The City," which is about the futility of the geographical cure for chronic restlessness: "Now that you have decided you are through / with this place, you've wrecked your life everywhere." And

1. Mason, *Ludlow*, 223.

2. All poetry quotations from Mason are taken from the individual first-edition volumes listed in the bibliography.

as Mason has his character Maggie Gresham say in his long poem "The Country I Remember" (from the eponymous collection, 1996), "I saw how fragile love is, / how easy to uproot from my place, / how hard to plant again."

Mason has done pretty much the opposite of what Maggie describes here, re-creating his life and art by an ever-deepening return to places and their stories, including the stories he himself invents about them. In *The Buried Houses*, Mason was still finding his legs as a writer; the technique is sometimes awkward or indecisive and subject matter often has more to do with a sense of *dis*placement—the displacement of expats in Greece, where Mason has spent considerable time and which comes up often in his writing, or that of the author himself, in his poems about the breakup of his first marriage: "It's strange what we can make ourselves believe. / Memory saves; recrimination uses / every twisted syllable of the past" ("Disclosure"). He came into his own as a poet with his second collection, *The Country I Remember*, three-quarters of which is taken up with the long title poem, a first-person narrative told in twelve alternating sections by two of Mason's ancestors: Lt. John Mitchell, who fought in the Civil War, and Mitchell's daughter Maggie Gresham. Mitchell, who tells his story retrospectively, in 1918, recounts his experience at the Battle of Chickamauga and his role in Union soldiers' escape from Libby Prison in Richmond, Virginia. Maggie Gresham narrates her own story in 1956, when she is an old woman. She describes how she eventually escaped from being an unmarried daughter who took care of her aging father and mother, running off and settling in Los Angeles. While Mitchell was a man of action, Maggie is introspective and reads poetry; her words about herself could apply to Mason:

> I learned that I must first talk to myself,
> retelling stories, muttering a few
> remembered lines of verse, to make the earth
> substantial and to bring the sunlight back.

She is "here to be a voice." It seems that writing this long poem was concurrent with Mason's discovery of his roots and the consummation of his apprenticeship as a poet.

Anyone who knows Mason's writing knows that he loves Greece, its language and culture.[3] Modern Greek poets such as Seferis and Cavafy are important to him. And there have been many poems set in Greece, in *Buried*

---

3. See Mason's memoir *News from the Village*.

Houses and *Arrivals*, as well as in *Sea Salt* (2014) and in the "New Poems" section of *The Sound: New and Selected Poems* (2018). It is interesting that Mason, whose family roots have been so central to his work, should have this other side—a wanderlust, including a pull toward the expat's existence. Greece in Mason's poems is both Epicurean and Homeric; it is an image of intense sensual presence and unreflective vitality—part of his drive to "feel more alive in [his] own skin," as he puts it in *Ludlow*. Apparently then, Greece—and later, Tasmania—for Mason represents a different, personal kind of rootedness. One of the main characters in *Ludlow*, Louis Tikas, is from Crete, and his Greekness and that of others in the miners' camp is a main feature of the story. Mason expresses his attachment to Greece through Tikas:

> he missed the sea,
> the tears of an eternity of men,
> the peacefulness of swimming under water.
>
> He missed the smell of grass in autumn rain,
> the sacks of dripping goat cheese hung from rafters,
> the words like *thálassa* and *ouranós*
> that felt to him much weightier than English.

As a poem in *Arrivals* about Mason's return to where he lived in Greece several years earlier explains, "it wasn't the loss of time or friends that moved me / but the small survivals I was here to mark," such as a plank bench under a cypress, "only a small plank bench, but quite enough" ("Kalamitsi")—enough, because needs were few. Things as they were and are is enough. Mason's Greece is not Hellenistic or classical; it is intense but simple, like the lives of his ancestors in Colorado. For Mason as for all people from the West, Greece is also the font of the ancient craft of poetry. A poem called "The Session," in *Arrivals*, alludes to this when the narrator responds to a psychotherapist's advice to socialize more and write less:

> I almost founder on his solid fears,
> until uplifted by the undertow
> of voices whispering for three thousand years.

Mason's aesthetic, like his image of Greece, eschews abstraction in favor of direct experience.

Another recurrent theme in Mason, related to roots and uprootedness, is memory and duration. Clearly events and people do not last very long, but memory and memorials—stories, in short—*do* last, at least relatively. Many of his poems reenact the fluid interplay between perception of the present and the ghosts of the past: "The furnace blows a warming reverie / where I drop anchor somewhere in the woods / with a girl I haven't seen for twenty years." But there is the awareness that memory's prolongation of time and experience is itself ephemeral, vaporous: "The years slow down and look about for shelter / far from forests and far from summer ponds: / the mind ghosting out in a shoal of stars" ("The Pond"). As Maggie Gresham puts it in "The Country I Remember":

> The lamplit face upon the swaying glass
> was all that I would ever know of truth.
> When Mama snuffed the lamp, my other face
> retreated to the land of passing shadows.

It seems likely that Mason's concern with memory and rootedness—his sense of urgency about it—is related to or intensified by the trauma of losing his older brother to a climbing accident when the brother was only twenty-eight years old. As Mason wrote in "Small Elegies," in *Buried Houses*: "My hands still felt, from earlier that day, / the tension of my brother's weight on the rope."

Mason has written many poems, as well as a prose memoir that was originally published in the *Hudson Review*, about his brother's death. Mason and his other brother and his father returned to the scene of the oldest brother's death and cremation that had taken place a year earlier:

> Yet after the year of weather
> tiny pieces of my brother's bone
> still lay in clefts of rock.
> We found them under our hands,
> cupping them once again in wonder
> at what the giants left us. ("A Motion We Cannot See")

With an experience such as this, it would be impossible not to be aware that memory and roots themselves are ultimately transient. As Wordsworth and others have noted, we erect tombs to prolong memory of the dead even as we are aware that the tombs themselves won't last. Mason's trauma of losing his brother heightened his sense of the impermanence of things, and of the phantasmagoric quality of memory that preserves the dead and the fleeting: "A second nature rises from the past, / just like the first in that it will not last, / and grips you as it slips free of your grasp" ("The Picketwire"). And the memory of that life is too subtle and protean to be captured in language:

> I live in a world too full of elegies,
> and find no compensation in these lines,
> nor can they map where memory begins
> its restoration under winter skies. ("Letter to No Address")

Mason quotes Darwin in the epigraph to his poem "New Zealand Letter" (in *Arrivals*): "Nothing, not even the wind that blows, is so unstable as the level of the crust of the earth." The poem depicts how "this metamorphic world" travels like the traveler himself, so that even in moving across the earth's surface, in this age of mass tourism, where "the spillage of spoiled empires everywhere / rumbles ashore like the redundant surf," in our frenetic movement we might forget that the earth itself is also moving under our very feet. Earth is "the sort of matter that endures / by changing." Consequently, as Mason says in the poem "The Dream of Arrival," we are "always preparing to arrive." In this poem, which alludes to Cavafy's poem on journeying to Ithaca, the speaker describes his voyage back to Ithaca, an archetypal story of return, only to realize when he does arrive that he "did not know the land."

> Always preparing to arrive,
> I suffer the deaths of many friends,
> survive, surprised to be alive.
> My story's told, but never ends

Mason intentionally omits the closing punctuation; as in Cavafy's poem, inconclusiveness is the nature of the journey.

So, Mason pays attention to what lasts beyond the individual's lifespan but acknowledges that even on a larger scale forms mutate and pass on. *The Country I Remember* includes a poem about a river in Colorado near which his ancestors settled (the same river appears also in *Ludlow*): "My people's home beside the Purgatoire / was brief—far briefer than our scattering." Even long-term settlements were once founded by people who had wandered there. In this case, the Spaniards who had been at the location before the coal mines attracted other settlers are now remembered only by the river's name, El Rio de las Animas Perdidas en Purgatorio, the river itself being an image of time's inexorable flow:

> No one recollects where the Spaniards died.
> A rescue party found their armored bones,

> thought their souls estranged from the love of God;
> so the river was named and flowed on past,
> bearing no knowledge of its wandering spirits,
> cupped to baptize newborns in the valley.

This theme has been present throughout Mason's work: "Much is known by now about the buried houses, / less about the people who uncovered them" ("The Buried Houses"); "The past I would recapture is a land / whose contours changed the further I moved out" ("Letter to No Address").

Mutability is a perennial, inevitable topic of poetry; the response to it is one of the defining characteristics of a poet. I have already mentioned that part of Mason's response has been to pay attention to the continuity of mnemonic forms: memory of the bonds between people, including their stories; memory of nature; memory of languages and poetic traditions. Yet all these forms are subject to loss and forgetting—a fact that for Mason has been especially tangible since losing his brother. From this it is a short hop to identifying with those who know no permanence, whose lives are haunted by a sense of not belonging anywhere. Many of Mason's poems identify with people who are dispossessed in one way or another. As he writes of a beggar in India: "What roll of the dice made me the healthy one / placing a rupee on his left arm's stump?" ("A Beggar of Chennai"). And another poem in *Arrivals*, a ballade, identifies with tramps, schizophrenics, and other outsiders:

> A Dunkin' Donuts denizen,
> Phil diagrammed conspiracies
> in which the country had a plan,
> contrived by top authorities,
> to generate our mass malaise.
> When I would ask him why or how,
> suspicion flickered in his eyes.
> I don't know where he's living now. ("Ballade at 3 A.M.")

As these quotations demonstrate, Mason does not choose these subjects to show off how compassionate he is or because of middle-class guilt. He uses the craft to give these experiences a name and a voice.

I have mentioned that Mason was drawn to the Ludlow story since he was young. The two main characters of *Ludlow*—which is an engrossing read from start to finish—are Louis Tikas and Luisa Mole. He is an immigrant from Crete, she is the daughter of a Welshman and a Mexican woman. Tikas is a historical figure, killed by state militia during the Ludlow massacre; Luisa, an orphan from age twelve who is taken on by a middle-class family as a helper and nurse, is Mason's invention. Mason has written novels and has worked in film production, and his sense of character development shows it: both these characters make a vivid impression. Such outsiders and immigrants inhabit Mason's poetry like personas for his own sense of loss:

> How long, O Lord, how long
> must one man journey till he finds his home?

And:

> Their lives are part of my life's inventory;
> my role grows smaller when I glimpse the whole.
> Today I pocketed a lump of coal.
> These are the facts, but facts are not the story.

This drive to use poetry to explore human lives on the margins, or simply people without a voice or sense of belonging, has been in Mason's work since the start. In *The Buried Houses*, for instance, there is a poem about a disillusioned middle-aged divorcée from Chicago who lives in Greece and is a tour guide for American students. The poem depicts her loneliness in contrast to the students' hopefulness and camaraderie: "Why should they want to know / one's hair grays, one's husband leaves, one's tongue / turns to stone?" ("The Nightingales of Andrítsena"). She is an uprooted expat, dissociated from the traumas of her past: "I do not think I have let myself be young. / I am a woman whose father committed suicide / in Chicago in 1939." "The Collector's Tale," an eight-page narrative poem in *Arrivals*, is about Foley, an American-Indian alcoholic and seller of Indian artifacts. The story is told by another collector who has known Foley for just two months. Foley shows up one night at the narrator's home, drunk, having just bludgeoned to death (with a souvenir buffalo bone) another dealer named Rasher. He tells how he hated Rasher for being a white guy who sold phony Indian artifacts: "The stuff is fucking new, / pure Disneyland, not even off the Rez." Rasher had shown Foley a horrific item: "a black man's head with eyes sewn shut— / . . . a metal ashtray planted in the skull"—and become so enraged over it he went to "some Yuppie bar / that charged a fortune for its cheapest bourbon," where he becomes further enraged by watching all the after-work yuppies who live "on bones / of other people." Mason's method here is typical of his narratives: out of Foley's speech he creates a convincing character, backed up with naturalistic description. Here is Foley from the outside:

> I still see him, round as a medicine ball
> with a three-day beard, wearing his ripped jeans
> and ratty, unlaced Nikes without socks.
> I see him searching through two empty packs
> and casting them aside despite my scowl,
> opening a third, lighting up—he careens
> into my kitchen, leaving boozy tracks.

These rhymed stanzas of the narrator are interspersed with Foley's blank-verse lines, a strategy that works well for this poem since it sets off Foley's speech as a drunken rant.

Mason has included longer narrative poems in all his volumes to date (*Ludlow* is one long narrative poem, with no lyrics). His penchant for this genre was evident already in *The Buried Houses*, which includes four narrative poems of three pages or more: "The Nightingales of Andrítsena," mentioned above; "The Next Place," which is about a traveling charlatan who sells bogus remedies and beauty lotions and is run out of town; "Spooning," about a small-town old man, who relates his memory of a girl who became a famous actress; and "Blackened Peaches," in which a western pioneer woman tells her story of hardship and loss, including the death of her husband. These all show clear signs of Frost's influence, and Mason himself has stated that Frost is his favorite American poet. Narrative poems after this first book, while still indebted to Frost, are more clearly Mason's own.

Interestingly, all of Mason's narratives are in the first person—until *Ludlow*, which is told in the third person. Like Frost or Browning, Mason often discovers what he most wants to say by speaking in the voice of someone other than himself. Mason and other recent poets have written in defense of the verse narrative; as Mason says in the afterword of *Ludlow*: "Narrative verse is not inherently harder to read than narrative prose. In the right hands, verse actually has more clarity, drive and economy than prose, and it can offer literary pleasures of a sort unavailable in other genres."[4] It seems obvious that there are advantages to stories in verse—to me the wonder is that this would have ever come into question. The decline of verse narrative in the twentieth century may have had something to do with people no longer reading aloud to each other. As every poetry lover knows, poetry isn't static print: it is a vibrating column of air. Our lungs

4. Mason, *Ludlow*, 228.

resuscitate the words on the page. In *Ludlow* the meter is inseparable from the storytelling:

> From the naked bed of a Denver whore
> named Alice—weazened and tubercular—
> Ilias Spantidakis moved back in
> to his American skin and his new name,
> from leading man in Greek to character
> in English who confused the tenses, lost
> the proper names for abstract principles
> and left some articles to faith.

Mason tells his story in a plain realistic manner (there are few metaphors or similes in his narrative poems)—with the blend of American speech rhythms and blank verse that he has mastered. In the process, he demonstrates why verse is still an excellent medium for narrative.

Stories can dramatize conflict arising from contrasting characters and paradoxes of characters' own temperaments. Mason does this well. In *Ludlow*, the gradual transition from the initial introduction of the main characters; to the establishment of their various story threads; to the slow buildup of tension between the coal company and the Baldwin-Flats security agency on one hand and the strikers on the other—while the individual stories, especially those of Tikas and Luisa, continue to spin out against the larger background—all of this is deftly and unobtrusively handled. The reader is drawn into the collective story of the miners' strike and the personal destinies of the characters, convinced of the connections.

Ludlow combines historical fact with personal destiny in a way only fiction can do. Mason's knack for identifying with and interest in outsiders and immigrants, which I discussed earlier, bears fruit in the creation of *Ludlow*'s two main characters, Tikas and Luisa (Mason perhaps chose her name to echo "Louis," so that she represents the invisible face of his more public existence). Tikas's real name was Ilias Spantidakis. He lived through a civil war back in his native Crete. He is intelligent and literate, and works at a coffee shop in Trinidad, Colorado, reading the newspaper to customers. He is in America for economic reasons, not because he really wants to be. Only when he visits the prostitutes does he feel truly alive; otherwise he is "uncertain of his skin." The narrator of *Ludlow*, who occasionally steps out of the story to reflect, offers:

> What does it mean—nation of immigrants?
> What are the accents, fables, voices of roads,

the tall tales told by the smallest desert plants?
Even the wind in the barbed wire goads
me into making lines, fencing my vagrant thought.
A story is the language of desire.
A journey home is never what it ought
to be.
　　A land of broken glass. Of gunfire.

Luisa Mole's story runs parallel to Tikas's—they meet only toward the end and in passing, close to the time the massacre takes place. Her father, John Mole, has died in a mining explosion, and her mother died before that. We follow Luisa as she goes to live as a nanny and housekeeper with the Reeds, a middle-class family with five children. Long narrative poems rise and fall in intensity. Mason knows how to pace a story and heighten the intensity when it's called for, such as this scene, when Luisa Mole is newly adjusting to having lost her parents. She is living with a miner and his wife until she is taken in by the Reeds:

Out of the rockfolds, the scrub, the deep sky,
out of the junipers that loosed the dark
when the sun crept over the mountaintops,
out of the mouths and tipples of the mines
where men still worked, inquest or no inquest,
where coke ovens glowed a stone inferno,
out of the train that wailed to Trinidad
and back to Denver with its load of news

came the sound that was not a sound, a muted
scratching for life.

At the end of *Ludlow*, the author fantasizes over what might have become of Luisa, imagining her still alive in the 1970s, sitting alone in a coffee shop, not really belonging anywhere. She never had her own family, remaining *la huerfana*, the orphan, to the end: "She could give and give / and make of giving something of a home . . . / all she knew for certain she was good at ever."

IT SEEMS IRONIC THAT Mason, a poet so intent on searching for deeply felt roots, moved to Tasmania, on the other side of the world from Colorado.

Some of the poetry he has published since *Ludlow* may provide clues as to where the move fits in the arc of Mason's work as a whole.

Sea Salt was Mason's first collection of shorter poems after *Arrivals* in 2004. His verse novel, *Ludlow*, and a memoir on Mason's time in and connection to Greece, *News from the Village*, as well as a collection of poetry criticism, were published in the meantime; and four years after *Sea Salt*, his *New and Selected Poems* came out from Red Hen Press. Mason has also written libretti for the composer Lori Laitman—an operatic version of *The Scarlet Letter* and a libretto for an oratorio, *Vedem*, based on the experiences of children at the concentration camp of Terezin—and a libretto for a one-act opera about the lives of Picasso and Gertrude Stein in Paris under the Nazis, to music by Tom Cipullo. An opera based on *Ludlow* (also by Laitman) debuted in 2015. Another book of narrative poems, called *Davey McGravy: Tales for Children and Adult Children*, came out from Paul Dry Books in 2015. Add to this that from 2010 to 2014 he was the poet laureate of Colorado, teaching at Colorado College, and traveling back and forth between Colorado and Oregon to be with his new wife Chrissy Mason, aka the poet Cally Conan-Davies, and it's easy to see that Mason has been living the full life. His and Chrissy's move to Tasmania opened a new chapter in his life and work.

Sea Salt is permeated by the themes and imagery of love, death, and the night, as well as the sea. *Arrivals*, too, as Gregory Dowling notes in his monograph on Mason,[5] was full of marine imagery, expressing an oceanic wish to be free of the self:

> That's how a lifetime passes,
> closing, re-closing the wound,
> a million stiches *[sic]* tied in time
> denying and re-denying
>
> until you learn to let
> it lie and let
> it weep,
> and open. ("Lieutenant Mason")

The title of *Sea Salt* fits its contents well: human beings are like sea salt, more porous and solvent than the ego would have us believe. A poem that lists various kinds of striving, socially approved behavior, and applauded achievement concludes that all those things are nothing compared

5. Dowling, *David Mason*, 82.

> to the auricles and sheaths,
> spikelets and seedheads of an ordinary
> end-of-summer clump of roadside grass. ("Incantation")

This resembles the conclusion that Antonio Machado reached when he said that all philosophies are gibberish compared to the eloquence of wind.

Death is a main character in *Sea Salt*. It first appears in the book with a narrative, "The Fawn," about a cousin who came to stay with Mason's family when he was a boy, and an incident when a neighborhood dog mortally injured a fawn, which the cousin tried to save in the family garage. Major changes—starting in 1963, the year of Kennedy's assassination, and extending to the poet's parents' breakup—are linked to the fawn's life-and-death moment:

> The years are a great winnowing of lives,
> but we had knelt together by the fawn
> and felt the silence intervene.

And there are poems about the infirmity and death of Mason's parents, as in the poem "Fathers and Sons," which opens with a universal and humbling real-life experience: assisting an old parent to use the toilet. Mason transforms the event with just the right dose of humor:

> How he had wiped my bottom
> half a century ago, and how
> I would repay the favor
> if he would only sit.

It is the most delicate and tender bathroom humor imaginable. But the father doesn't understand the son's laughter at that moment, and is prevented by Alzheimer's from saying so. The poem concludes:

> Somewhere
> a man of dignity would not be laughed at.
> He could not see
> it was the crazy dance
> that made me laugh
> trying to make him sit
> when he wanted to stand.

If there is a more touching middle-age-son-with-his-frail-father poem than this, I haven't read it yet.

Animals suffer the loss of their dead, but human beings—the beings that question being, as Heidegger memorably put it—think and wonder about them as well. Death, like love and the night, wakes us from the dream of what we call daily life. It reminds us we're salt in the sea. "The Future," a poem in the second section of *Sea Salt*, remarks:

> We know we are nothing,
> forgetting our names
> or the names of the cities,
> the nothing we know as we know
> the light on a window.

Mason's lyrical poems, such as this one, often play at the edges of a kind of agnostic or atheistic negative theology, circling around the unsayable:

> Others grew up with chrism, incense, law,
> but I was exiled from the start to stare
> at lightning hurled from the sky
> into a lake that revealed only itself. ("A Thorn in the Paw")

As the title poem at the end of *Sea Salt* concludes:

> The days are made of hours,
> hours of instances,
> and none of them are ours.
> The sand blows through the fences.
> Light darkens on the grass.
> This too shall come to pass.

That last line, which is repeated twice in the poem, means "This will happen as well," but it also recalls the saying "This too shall pass," meaning "This will be over eventually," which we say or are told when we're miserable in one way or another. The sense of acquiescence and imminence, of anticipated and occasionally realized release, runs through much of Mason's poetry, but seems particularly concentrated in *Sea Salt*.

The middle of *Sea Salt* contains a sea-change in Mason's life and work, leaping into new love with the playful "Sarong Song," in quatrains of alternating tetrameter and trimeter. After this, scattered throughout the rest of the collection, there is a string of love poems that seem to embody the release that *Arrivals* had craved. "The Soul Fox," for instance, is one of those short, perfect lyrics that gives the appearance of having come out whole; the life experience that triggered it and the experience of the poem itself are indivisibly joined:

160

> Write.
> Let the white page bear the mark,
> then melt with joy upon the dark.

This poem, dedicated to Chrissy Mason, condenses the fundamental insight that love, which always lives in the present, gives lovers night-vision. After seeing a fox in the yard, knowing that the footprints left behind in the snow will melt, the speaker says:

> we who saw
> his way of finding out, his night
> of seeking, know what we have seen
> and are the better for it.

In "Night and My Love," the unknowing knowledge of love is synonymous with night, where, as with death, our daytime identity is left behind:

> Night, I beg you, night,
> anoint me with anonymity,
> annul my neediness, my expectations,
> and let my love sleep on and wake
> annealed, anew . . .

The sonnet "Another Thing" confirms the sense that new love has helped the speaker to let go of artificial unity and cohesiveness:

> The others are one thing. They know they are.
> One compass needle. They have found their way
> and navigate by perfect cynosure.
> Go wreck yourself once more against the day
> and wash up like a bottle on the shore,
> lucidity and salt in all you say.

There's the salt again, and the marine imagery, which in Mason's writing links back to his youthful discoveries during a year in Greece, living on the bay of Kalamitsi. I don't know what Mason's own thoughts are about his move to Tasmania, so this is mere conjecture, but it strikes me that there is poetic consistency in the choice of his new home, surrounded like Greece by salt water, in this case the Southern Ocean. Like Greece, Tasmania for Mason is a place of origins and visceral belonging. As he stated in a 2021 online interview from Tasmania, he has felt that waking up there at dawn is like stirring on the first day of the creation.[6] This suggests that there

6. "Poems on Nature #9," part 2.

is something of a Yeatsian wish for an awareness as cold and wanton as dawn in Mason's expatriation. The human place in Mason's work appears wherever people are alive and present in their own skins.

Acknowledgments

A LL of the pieces in this book have been previously published, in earlier versions, in print or online journals. My thanks to the editors of the *Contemporary Poetry Review, Hudson Review, Los Angeles Review of Books,* and *Temenos Academy Review* for getting them into print to begin with. Special thanks to John Carey, general editor of *Temenos Academy Review,* whose insight, sensitivity, learning, and editorial rigor have left their mark on several of the pieces in this book. This book is dedicated to him. I thank Norman Jope, Paul Scott Derrick, and Catherine E. Byfield, editors of *The Companion to Richard Berengarten,* for help in revising my essay on Richard Berengarten for that volume. My thanks also to Richard Ramsbotham and Stephen Overy, for mediating my contact with Gwen Watkins and Conrad Watkins for permission to quote from Vernon Watkins. I am grateful as well to Richard Berengarten and David Mason, for easing the way in getting permission to quote from their writings.

Finally, I thank my wife Daphne Lull for her companionship and support, as well as her invaluable feedback on all my work.

I am grateful as well to publishers and individuals that made it possible for me to quote from texts in this book: Fair-use quotations from Edwin Muir are taken from *Collected Poems* (London: Faber and Faber, 1984); "Giuseppe Ungaretti and the Image of Desolation" from *Selected Poems: A Bilingual Edition* by Giuseppe Ungaretti, translated by Andrew Frisardi. Translation and Introduction copyright © 2002 by Andrew Frisardi. Reprinted by permission of Farrar, Straus and Giroux. All Rights Reserved; Extracts from Vernon Watkins, *Collected Poems* (Ipswich: Golgonooza Press, 1986), are printed here with permission of Gwen Watkins and

Acknowledgments

Conrad Watkins, and of Golgonooza Press. Copyright © Gwen Watkins, 1986; Extracts from Kathleen Raine, *Collected Poems* (Ipswich, England: Golgonooza Press, 2000), are printed here with permission of the Literary Estate of Kathleen Raine. Copyright © Brian Keeble, 2000; Fair-use quotations from Peter Russell, "Albae Meditatio," are taken from *Poesie dal Valdarno* (Florence, Italy: Pietro Chegai Editore, 1999), and "A Celebration," from *Elemental Discourses* (Salzburg, Austria: Salzburg University Press, 1981); John Haines, excerpts from "In the Forest without Leaves," "Meditation on a Skull Carved in Crystal," and "Night" from *The Owl in the Mask of the Dreamer: Collected Poems*. Copyright © 1990, 1996 by John Haines. Reprinted with the permission of The Permissions Company, LLC on behalf of Graywolf Press, Minneapolis, Minnesota, www.graywolfpress. org; Extracts from Richard Berengarten, *The Blue Butterfly* (3rd edition; Exeter: Shearsman Books, 2011) are printed here with permission of the author, and of Shearsman Books Ltd. Copyright © Richard Berengarten, 2006, 2008, 2011; Extracts from David Mason, *Buried Houses*, *The Country I Remember*, and *Arrivals* (Ashland, Oreg.: Story Line Press, 1991, 1996, 2004), and *Ludlow* and *Sea Salt* (Pasadena, Calif.: Red Hen Press, 2007, 2014), are printed here with permission of the author, and of Red Hen Press, Copyright © David Mason, 1991, 1996, 2004, 2007, 2014.

BIBLIOGRAPHY

Alighieri, Dante. *Convivio: A Dual-Language Critical Edition.* Edited and translated by Andrew Frisardi. Cambridge: Cambridge University Press, 2018.

Arendt, Hannah. *Eichmann in Jerusalem: A Report on the Banality of Evil.* London: Faber and Faber, 1963.

Baldini, Antonio, and Emilio Cecchi. *Carteggio: 1911–1959.* Edited by Maria Clotilde Angelini and Marta Bruscia. Rome: Storia e Letteratura, 2003.

Berengarten, Richard. *The Blue Butterfly.* Cambridge: Salt, 2006.

———. *Ceri Richards and Dylan Thomas: Keys to Transformation.* London: Enitharmon, 1981.

Bezner, Kevin, and Kevin Walzer, eds. *The Wilderness of Vision: On the Poetry of John Haines.* Brownsville, OR: Story Line, 1996.

Blake, William. *Blake: Complete Writings.* Edited by Geoffrey Keynes. Oxford: Oxford University Press, 1966.

Cambon, Glauco. *Giuseppe Ungaretti.* New York: Columbia University Press, 1967.

Carey, John. "Learning, Imagination and Belief." In *The Cambridge History of Ireland,* vol. 1, *600–1550,* edited by Brendan Smith, 47–75. Cambridge: Cambridge University Press, 2018.

Cary, Joseph. *Three Modern Italian Poets: Saba, Ungaretti, Montale.* Chicago: University of Chicago Press, 1993.

Coomaraswamy, A. K. "Eastern Religions and Western Thought." *Review of Religion* 6 (1942) 134–35.

Cullingford, Elizabeth. *Yeats, Ireland, and Fascism.* London: Macmillan, 1981.

Dowling, Gregory. *David Mason: A Critical Introduction.* West Chester, PA: Story Line, 2013.

Ellmann, Richard. *The Identity of Yeats.* 2nd ed. London: Faber and Faber, 1975.

———. *Yeats: The Man and the Masks.* New York: Dutton, 1948.

Haines, John. *For the Century's End: Poems, 1990–1999.* Pacific Northwest Poetry Series. Seattle: University of Washington Press, 2001.

———. *The Owl in the Mask of the Dreamer: Collected Poems.* St. Paul, MN: Graywolf, 1993.

———. *The Stars, the Snow, the Fire: Twenty-five Years in the Northern Wilderness.* St. Paul, MN: Graywolf, 2000.

———. "The Theme of Loss, of Sorrow and Redemption in Gilgamesh." Lecture, ca. 1999. Unpublished ten-page typescript.

Hillman, James. *Re-Visioning Psychology*. New York: Harper and Row, 1975.

Jung, C. G. *Synchronicity: An Acausal Connecting Principle*. Translated by R. F. C. Hull. Princeton, NJ: Princeton University Press, 1973.

Keeble, Brian. "An Interview." In *These Bright Shadows: The Poetry of Kathleen Raine*, 5–38. Brooklyn, NY: Angelico, 2020.

———. *Kathleen Raine: Poetic Imagination and the Vision of Reality*. Temenos Academy Papers 28. London: Temenos Academy, 2008.

———. "Myself I Must Remake." In *Conversing with Paradise*, 81–107. Ipswich, England: Golgonooza, 2003.

———. *Vernon Watkins: Inspiration as Poetry, Poetry as Inspiration*. Temenos Academy Papers 19. London: Temenos Academy, 2002.

Lakhani, M. Ali. *Faith and Ethics: The Vision of the Ismaili Imamat*. London: Tauris, 2018.

Loloi, Parvin. "Sufi Elements in Peter Russell's 'Albae Meditatio.' " *Swansea Review* 19 (2000) 58–78.

Mason, David. *Arrivals*. Brownsville, OR: Story Line, 2004.

———. *The Buried Houses*. Brownsville, OR: Story Line, 1991.

———. *The Country I Remember*. Brownsville, OR: Story Line, 1996.

———. *Ludlow: A Verse-Novel*. Pasadena, CA: Red Hen, 2007.

———. *News from the Village: Aegean Friends*. Pasadena, CA: Red Hen, 2010.

———. "Poems on Nature #9," part 2. Conversation between Al Basile, David Mason, and Cally Conan-Davies. Available on www.youtube.com/watch?v=fKjtIw50K4w (accessed February 20, 2022).

———. *Sea Salt: Poems of a Decade, 2004–2014*. Pasadena, CA: Red Hen, 2014

McElwee, Joshua J. "Francis Criticizes Traditionalist Catholics Who 'Safeguard the Ashes' of the Past." *National Catholic Reporter*, June 2, 2019. Available online at www.ncronline.org/news/vatican/francis-criticizes-traditionalist-catholics-who-safeguard-ashes-past (accessed February 23, 2022).

Milton, John. *The Portable Milton*. Edited by Douglas Bush. London: Penguin, 1976.

Muir, Edwin. *An Autobiography*. 1954. Repr., London: Methuen, 1964.

———. *Collected Poems*. London: Faber and Faber, 1984.

———. *Essays on Literature and Society*. 1949. 2nd ed., Cambridge, MA: Harvard University Press, 1965.

———. *The Estate of Poetry*. Foreword by Archibald MacLeish. Introduction by John Haines. 1962. New ed., St. Paul, MN: Graywolf, 1993.

———. *The Politics of King Lear*. New York: Haskell House, 1947.

———. *Selected Letters of Edwin Muir*. Edited by P. H. Butter. London: Hogarth, 1974.

Nasr, Seyyed Hossein. "Kathleen Raine and Tradition." *Temenos Academy Review* 7 (2004) 179–85.

Nicholson, R. A. *Studies in Islamic Mysticism*. Cambridge: Cambridge University Press, 1921.

Novalis. *Henry von Ofterdingen*. Translated by Palmer Hilty. Prospect Heights, IL: Waveland, 1990.

Oddo, Giusy. *Ungaretti: The Man and the Poet*. 2010. Available online at BiblioSofia, http://www.bibliosofia.net/Giusy_-_Ungaretti__saggio_.pdf (accessed February 22, 2022).

Plotinus. *Enneads*. Translated by Thomas Taylor. Westbury, England: Prometheus Trust, 2017.

Polk, Dora. *Vernon Watkins and the Spring of Vision*. Swansea, Wales: Christopher Davies, 1977.

Raine, Kathleen. *Autobiographies*. London: Skoob, 1991.

———. *Blake and Tradition*. 2 vols. London: Routledge & Kegan Paul, 1969.

———. *Collected Poems*. Ipswich, England: Golgonooza, 2000.

———. *Defending Ancient Springs*. London: Oxford University Press, 1967.

———. *The Human Face of God: William Blake and the Book of Job*. London: Thames & Hudson, 1982.

———. *India Seen Afar*. New York: George Braziller, 1990.

———. *The Inner Journey of the Poet and Other Papers*. Edited by Brian Keeble. London: George Allen & Unwin, 1982.

———. Interview with Brian Keeble. *Temenos Academy Review* 7 (2004) 27–58.

———. *That Wondrous Pattern: Essays on Poetry and Poets*. Edited and with an introduction by Brian Keeble. Preface by Wendell Berry. Berkeley, CA: Counterpoint, 2017.

———. "Thomas Taylor in England." In *Thomas Taylor the Platonist: Selected Writings*, edited by Kathleen Raine and George Mills Harper, 3–48. Bollingen Series 88. Princeton, NJ: Princeton University Press, 1969.

———. *The Underlying Order and Other Essays*. Edited and with an introduction by Brian Keeble. London: Temenos Academy, 2008.

———. *W. B. Yeats and the Learning of the Imagination*. Ipswich, England: Golgonooza, 1999.

———. *Yeats the Initiate: Essays on Certain Themes in the Work of W. B. Yeats*. Mountrath, Ireland: Dolmen; London: George Allen & Unwin, 1986.

Ramsbotham, Richard. *An Exact Mystery: The Poetic Life of Vernon Watkins*. N.p.: Choir, 2020.

Rebay, Luciano. "Jean Paulhan–Giuseppe Ungaretti: Carteggio, 1921–1968." *Forum Italicum: A Journal of Italian Studies* 21, no. 2 (1987) 305–19.

Rumens, Carol. "Poem of the Week: Story's End by Kathleen Raine." *The Guardian*, August 5, 2019.

Russell, Peter. *Elemental Discourses*. Salzburg, Austria: University of Salzburg Press, 1981.

———. *Image of Woman as a Figure of the Spirit*. Salzburg, Austria: University of Salzburg Press, 1992.

———. *My Wild Heart*. Salzburg, Austria: University of Salzburg Press, 1998.

———. *Poesie dal Valdarno*. Florence: Chegai, 1999.

———. *The Progress of the Soul*. Pian di Scò: n.p., 1992.

———. *Something About Poetry*. Salzburg, Austria: University of Salzburg Press, 1997.

———. *Venice Poems 1965*. Salzburg, Austria: University of Salzburg Press, 1995.

Sanesi, Roberto. "Vernon Watkins." *Temenos* 8 (1987) 102–25.

Santayana, George. *Three Philosophical Poets: Lucretius, Dante, and Goethe*. Cambridge, MA: Harvard University Press, 1944.

Shelley, Percy Bysshe. *Shelley*. Selected and introduced by Kathleen Raine. Harmondsworth, England: Penguin, 1973.

Ungaretti, Giuseppe. *Selected Poems*. Translated, annotated, and with an introduction by Andrew Frisardi. New York: Farrar, Straus & Giroux, 2002.

———. *Vita d'un uomo: Saggi e interventi*. Edited by Mario Diacono and Luciano Rebay. Milan: Mondadori, 1974.

————. *Vita d'un uomo: Tutte le poesie.* Edited by Leone Piccioni. Milan: Mondadori, 1969.

Watkins, Vernon. *Collected Poems.* Ipswich, England: Golgonooza, 1986.

————. *New Selected Poems.* Edited and introduced by Richard Ramsbotham. Foreword by Rowan Williams. Manchester: Carcanet, 2006.

————. *Vernon Watkins on Dylan Thomas and Other Poets and Poetry.* Foreword by Rowan Williams. Edited by Gwen Watkins and Jeff Towns. Cardigan, Wales: Parthian, 2013.

Wheelwright, Philip, ed. *The Presocratics.* New York: Odyssey, 1966.

Williams, Rowan, host. "Swansea's Other Poet." BBC broadcast on March 11, 2012. Available at www.bbc.co.uk/programmes/b01dow2t (accessed February 21, 2022).

Yeats, W. B. *Autobiographies.* Edited by William H. O'Donnell and Douglas N. Archibald. Vol. 3 of *Collected Works*, 14 vols., general editors Richard J. Finneran and George Mills Harper. New York: Scribner, 1999.

————. *The Collected Plays of W. B. Yeats.* New ed. New York: Macmillan, 1953.

————. *Collected Poems.* London: Macmillan, 1987.

————. *Essays and Introductions.* New York: Collier, 1968.

————. *Explorations.* Selected by Mrs. W. B. Yeats. London: Macmillan, 1962.

————. *The Letters of W. B. Yeats.* Edited by Allan Wade. London: Rupert Hart-Davis, 1954.

————. *Mythologies.* New York: Collier, 1969.

————. *The Poems.* Edited by Daniel Albright. London: Everyman's, 1992.

————. *The Variorum Edition of the Poems of W. B. Yeats.* Edited by Peter Allt and Russell K. Alspach. London: Macmillan, 1957.

————. *A Vision.* 1st ed. London: Werner and Laurie, 1926.

————. *A Vision.* 2nd ed. 1938. Repr., New York: Collier, 1966.